METAVERSE 2023 INVESTING

BEGINNERS TO ADVANCE, MONETISE TRENDS, FASHION, COINS, GAMES, NFTS, WEB3, DIGITAL ASSETS, REAL ESTATE, VIRTUAL REALITY (VR), AND CRYPTOCURRENCY INVESTMENTS

THE META-VERSE

© Copyright 2023 by (United Arts Publishing, England.) - All rights reserved.

This document is geared towards providing exact and reliable information in regard to the topic and issue covered. The publication is sold with the idea that the publisher is not required to render accounting, officially permitted, or otherwise, qualified services. If advice is necessary, legal or professional, a practised individual in the profession should be ordered. From a Declaration of Principles which was accepted and approved equally by a Committee of the American Bar Association and a Committee of Publishers and Associations.

In no way is it legal to reproduce, duplicate, or transmit any part of this document in either electronic means or in printed format. Recording of this publication is strictly prohibited and any storage of this document is not allowed unless with written permission from the publisher. All rights reserved.

The information provided herein is stated to be truthful and consistent, in that any liability, in terms of inattention or otherwise, by any usage or abuse of any policies, processes, or directions contained within is the solitary and utter responsibility of the recipient reader. Under no circumstances will any legal responsibility or blame be held against the publisher for any reparation, damages, or monetary loss due to the information herein, either directly or indirectly. Respective authors own all copyrights not held by the publisher.

The information herein is offered for informational purposes solely, and is universal as so. The presentation of the information is without contract or any type of guarantee assurance. The trademarks that are used are without any consent, and the publication of the trademark is without permission or backing by the trademark owner. All trademarks and brands within this book are for clarifying purposes only and are the owned by the owners themselves, not affiliated with this document.

WANT FREE NEW BOOK LAUNCHES?

EMAIL US AT:
mindsetmastership@gmail.com

SCAN ME FOR A BONUS

https://bonus.mindsetmastership.com/metaverse-2023-investing

ARE YOU READY TO JOIN IN ON THE NEW CRYPTO REVOLUTION?

Introducing *Investing in Metaverse, NFTs, Blockchain, and DeFi: Taking Advantage Of The New Crypto Economy*

IN THIS FREE BONUS GUIDE DISCOVER:

- Metaverse - 5 Most Lucrative Projects in 2023!
- NFTs - Top 10 Trending NFT Fractionalization Projects in 2023!
- Blockchain - 5 Cryptocurrencies Under $1 Skyrocketing in 2023!
- DeFi - 6 DEXs That Will Revolutionize the Crypto Market in 2023!

PLUS BONUS NEW FREE BOOK RELEASES!

SCAN THE QR CODE TO CLAIM YOUR FREE BONUS NOW!

https://bonus.mindsetmastership.com/metaverse-2023-investing

JOIN OUR NFT CRYPTO ART ENTREPENUER POWER GROUP

To help reinforce the learning's from our books, I strongly suggest you join our well-informed powerhouse community on Facebook.

Here, you will connect and share with other like-minded people to support your journey and help you grow.

Follow and Like our Facebook Page
to get the latest updates on our new book releases:
https://www.facebook.com/nfttrending/

To Join Our Personal Support Group Go To:
https://www.facebook.com/groups/nfttrending/

OUR OTHER BOOKS ON AMAZON

Follow us on Amazon:
NFT Trending Crypto Art

Decentralized Finance (DeFi) Investment Guide; Platforms, Exchanges, Lending, Borrowing, Options Trading, Flash Loans & Yield-Farming: Bull & Bear of Bitcoin ... (Decentralized Finance (DeFi) Books Book 2)

Decentralized Finance DeFi 2022 Investing Guide, Lend, Trade, Save Bitcoin & Ethereum do Business in Cryptocurrency Peer to Peer (P2P) Staking, Flash Loans ... (Decentralized Finance (DeFi) Books Book 3)

NFT (Non Fungible Tokens), Guide; Buying, Selling, Trading, Investing in Crypto Collectibles Art. Create Wealth and Build Assets: Or Become a NFT Digital ... to Advanced The Ultimate Handbook Book 1)

NFT Investing for Beginners to Advanced, Make Money; Buy, Sell, Trade, Invest in Crypto Art, Create Digital Assets, Earn

Passive income in Cryptocurrency, ... to Advanced The Ultimate Handbook Book 2)

NFT (Non-Fungible Token) Investing Guide Create Your Crypto Art Marketplace Platform: Learn to, Buy, Trade, Hold, The Most Valuable Digital NFT Art Collections ... to Advanced The Ultimate Handbook Book 3)

NFT (Non Fungible Tokens) Investing Guide for Beginners to Advance 2022 & Beyond : NFTs Handbook for Artists, Real Estate & Crypto Art, Buying, Flipping ... to Advanced The Ultimate Handbook 4)

Blockchain Investing; Bitcoin, Cryptocurrency, NFT, DeFi, Metaverse, Smart contracts, Distributed Ledgers, DAO, Web 3.0 & 5G: The Next Technology Revolution To Change Everything Ultimate Guide

Ethereum 2.0 Cryptocurrency Investing Book: A Beginners Guide to Invest in The Eth2 Crypto Merge, The Future Internet Money Millionaire Maker

CONTENTS

Introduction xv

1. WHAT IS THE METAVERSE? 1
   Features of the Metaverse 2
   Anchoring Concepts of the Metaverse 3
   Different Forms of the Metaverse 6
   Peeking Into the Metaverse Economy 12
   Key takeaways 14

2. HOW TO INVEST IN METAVERSE? 15
   Can You Invest in the Metaverse? 16
   Metaverse Categories to Invest 17
   Primary Ways to Invest in Metaverse 25
   Top Metaverse Investors 27
   Key takeaways 32

3. OPPORTUNITIES AND RISKS OF METAVERSE 33
   Opportunities Enable by the Metaverse 34
   Risks Enabled by the Metaverse 36
   Dispelling Metaverse Myths 38
   Economic Impact of Metaverse 40
   Lucrative Metaverse Jobs 42
   Open Metaverse 44
   Key takeaways 47

4. METAVERSE BUSINESS OPPORTUNITIES 49
   How Can Metaverse Help in Business 49
   Three Ways How Metaverse Will Transform Business Processes 52
   Business Opportunities 54
   Is Metaverse the Right Way to Go? 56
   Top 12 Metaverse Brands Selling Digital Products 58
   Key takeaways 62

5. METAVERSE DEVICES AND TECHNOLOGY — 65
- Metaverse Devices — 66
- Things to Consider When Selecting Your Metaverse Equipment — 67
- 7 Key Technologies Powering the Metaverse — 68
- The Industrial Metaverse — 71
- Automotive Industry to Include Metaverse — 72
- Metaverse Stirs Up Software Development — 73
- The Age of Revolution for Telcos — 74
- Key takeaways — 77

6. METAVERSE TRENDS AND PREDICTIONS — 79
- Metaverse Predictions to Lookout for in 2023 — 79
- The Emergence of Metaverse-Based Social Platforms and Communities — 80
- The Growth of the Metaverse Economy and the Emergence of Virtual Real Estate — 81
- What Businesses can Anticipate from the Metaverse in 2023 — 84
- Metaverse Development Companies in 2023 — 88
- Key takeaways — 92

7. THE METAVERSE AND THE FUTURE — 95
- Why the Metaverse is the Future — 95
- Metaverse: The Future of Work — 100
- Why Does it Matter that the Metaverse is Expanding? — 104
- The Metaverse in 2030 — 106
- Can Metaverse Live up to the Hype? — 109
- Key takeaways — 113

CONCLUSION — 115

INTRODUCTION

In the Metaverse, people communicate and participate in ways that would be impossible in the physical world. In the actual world, relationships and bonds aren't possible. The term "Metaverse" is commonly used to refer to a fully immersive and participatory digital world. As long as there have been science fiction stories and video games, the idea of a Metaverse has been floating around.

In science fiction literature, the depiction of the Metaverse is common. It is frequently portrayed as a virtual reality environment that can be accessed using some type of technology, such as a headset or other virtual reality equipment. It is a place where people may break free from the constraints of the actual world and simultaneously participate in both unique and exhilarating activities.

An example are those video games that commonly depict the Metaverse as a digital universe of their creation. Players can interact with one another and participate in various activities in this universe. These activities include the exploration of new places, the completion of missions, and participation in combat.

Introduction

The Metaverse concept has expanded thanks to the rapid growth of technology, going beyond the worlds of science fiction and virtual reality. It is gradually turning into an essential component of our day-to-day lives, which may be attributed, in large part, to the rapid development of technologies related to virtual reality as well as the expansion of online social interactions. It brings people from all around the world together in fascinating and original ways. It can change the face of many industries, from the arts and education to business.

The increase in social networking sites and the expansion of technology supporting virtual reality can be credited for the rise in the significance of the Metaverse. Virtual reality (VR) headsets and immersive environments have allowed people a more natural and tangible experience of the Metaverse than ever before due to technological breakthroughs in virtual reality (VR). At the same time, the explosion of social media and other online platforms has made it easy for individuals to connect and communicate with one another regardless of where they are physically located.

The advancements that paved the way for the Metaverse to become a natural part of our day-to-day lives have made this possible. Ongoing applications include:

- Online social communities
- Virtual reality events and conferences
- Online social games and experiences
- Online social communities

Over the next several years, we expect to see an increment in the number of companies and organizations studying the prospects offered by the Metaverse. The entertainment industry, education, and even business are potential areas that the Metaverse's revolution could significantly impact.

Introduction

When the Metaverse fully develops, it will be a fascinating new realm where people from all over the world can meet and converse. It should encourage new kinds of human contact and bring together individuals from all over the world. For instance, individuals who are not usually able to connect with others due to their location or physical limitation can use the Metaverse to communicate with others and participate in social and cultural activities.

Concurrently, the advent of the Metaverse raises a wide range of ethical and societal concerns that must be addressed and adequately handled. It is necessary to respond to questions and problems around privacy breaches and individual rights to virtual property. Inquiries into how the Metaverse may affect our interpersonal connections and sense of self are also included in the mandate. It will be essential to investigate these topics and find ways to balance the Metaverse's benefits and possible risks and challenges as it becomes more prevalent in mainstream culture. This will be accomplished by discovering ways to balance the Metaverse's benefits and the possible risks and challenges it could present.

This book's objective is to look at the numerous parts of the Metaverse in a way that is exhaustive and thought-provoking. We will investigate the planning and development of the Metaverse, possible uses and applications, and potential future repercussions for society by utilizing a mix of in-depth studies from industry professionals and examples from the real world.

We will start with the history of the Metaverse, beginning with its origins in works of science fiction literature and video games and then progressing to its present form as a technology constantly changing. In doing so, we will move from its past to the current form as a continually evolving technology. Subsequently, we will delve into the creation and development of the Metaverse, looking at the different technologies and platforms being leveraged to construct immersive and interactive virtual worlds.

We will also investigate the myriad uses and applications of the Metaverse by looking at how it is currently being used in diverse fields, including the entertainment industry, the educational system, and the business world. We cover how people can utilize the Metaverse to create innovative methods of interacting and working together, including the advantages and disadvantages of these uses.

We have researched the possible long-term implications of the Metaverse on human society. As a result of the expansion of the Metaverse, new ethical and sociological challenges have surfaced, the topic of the following conversation. Concerns about the invasion of privacy and infringements of rights to virtual property are among the relevant issues. We will also investigate the possibility that the Metaverse can affect our relationships and sense of self. We will further discuss in detail how the Metaverse may influence the future of human connection and communication.

As we progress through this book, a primary goals will be to provide a balanced and comprehensive view of the Metaverse, considering its potential and limitations. To do this, we must examine the Metaverse, including the potential benefits and drawbacks. Reading this book should help you come away with a deeper appreciation for the implications of the incredible technological progress we have made in our day. Ultimately, I hope you will grasp the concept completely.

Dear Reader,

As independent authors, it's often difficult to gather reviews compared with much bigger publishers.

Therefore, please leave a review on the platform where you bought this book.

KINDLE:

LEAVE A REVIEW HERE < click here >

Many thanks,

Author Team

1
WHAT IS THE METAVERSE?

When describing a virtual reality universe inhabited by millions of individuals, the phrase "Metaverse" was used initially in Neal Stephenson's 1992 science fiction novel, *Snow Crash*. Since then, the term has been widely used. Since its inception, the idea of the Metaverse has expanded to include not only the virtual reality but also augmented reality and mixed reality settings. These settings allow users to engage with one another and digital content in real-time.

The word "Metaverse" describes the shared virtual environment when augmented virtual reality meets physically persistent virtual space. Due to this impact, the Metaverse was born, which includes every imaginable online space in addition to augmented reality and the internet. Users can access this shared virtual environment and engage in conversation with one another in real-time by employing avatars and other forms of digital property.

The Metaverse will bring about sweeping changes in how we live, work, and communicate with one another and the environment around us. It can bring people together in previously imagined ways while it offers new opportunities for socialization, education, entertainment, and commerce.

In this chapter, we will examine the history of the Metaverse, its primary forms, as well as the essential characteristics that give it the distinction of being a one-of-a-kind and immersive digital realm. In addition, we will go into the foundational ideas of the Metaverse, such as identity, ownership, trade, and social interaction. We will also take a sneak peek at the Metaverse economy's current state and its potential for future growth.

Features of the Metaverse

The sensation of being "within" the virtual environment and having a powerful awareness of one's physical surroundings is referred to as immersion, one of the distinguishing characteristics of the Metaverse. This can be accomplished by utilizing images, high-quality audio, and the application of technology such as virtual or augmented reality.

Because it enables users to engage with one another and the environment in real-time, interactivity is another crucial aspect of the Metaverse. Activities like chatting, going on adventures, and competing in games with other people fall under this category.

The fact that the virtual environment and the activities that take place within it are maintained even when users are not actively participating is another essential characteristic of the Metaverse. Persistence refers to this aspect. Thanks to this feature, users can return to it later and pick up where they left off.

Scalability is another characteristics of the Metaverse. This allows a limitless number of users to access and explore the virtual environment simultaneously. This can be accomplished by utilizing servers and several other technologies to manage enormous data volumes and traffic.

The sensation of being in the company of other individuals, even while those individuals are not present, is referred to as "social presence." It's a vital feature of the Metaverse as a whole. This is accomplished by using avatars and other digital representations of users and utilizing social features such as chat and voice communication. It can also be achieved by using different digital representations of users.

The elements of the Metaverse, taken as a whole, make it possible for users to engage with one another and with digital environments in various ways, resulting in a singular and immersive experience.

Anchoring Concepts of the Metaverse

The Metaverse's anchoring concepts are a collection of guiding principles that determine how people engage with and learn from virtual worlds. These broader categories include identity and avatar design, virtual property and ownership, digital economies, government oversight, and regulation.

Identity and Avatar Creation

Users' conceptions of themselves and their avatars are fundamental to their experiences and interactions in the Metaverse. People in the Metaverse can make and personalize digital characters called "avatars" to stand in for them in various online environments. These avatars serve as a visual representation of the user and can be used to communicate and socialize with others in the Metaverse.

In the Metaverse, users can take many routes when making avatars. In some MMOGs, players can design their avatars from scratch, giving them unlimited freedom to express their unique personalities and interests in their online personas. VR systems may let you pick your skin tone, hairstyle, and wardrobe. One feature of metaverse platforms is the capacity to scan a user's physical appearance and import it into the virtual world, thereby providing a more lifelike representation of the user in the virtual environment.

Users can alter the avatar's visual appearance, actions, and behavior. Expressions, movements, and gestures are all part of this. Some Metaverse platforms even allow users to customize their avatars' voices and speech patterns.

Anchoring ideas of the Metaverse, identity, and avatar creation permit users to express themselves and establish a distinct online persona. People who aren't confident enough to be themselves out in the real world may find this enticing. In the Metaverse, users can try new identities and engage with others more genuinely and meaningfully.

Virtual Property and Ownership

Virtual property and ownership are fundamental to the Metaverse, affecting how people use digital goods. Users in the Metaverse can buy, sell, and barter with virtual commodities, real estate, and currencies.

Land, houses, shops, buildings, and personal possessions can all be considered "virtual property" in the Metaverse. These digital assets can be traded for real money in digital marketplaces, with prices based on supply and demand. Due to scarcity, some digital goods may be one-of-a-kind rarities that fetch a premium price.

In the Metaverse, a person's identity and avatar can be associated with forming a virtual property ownership system. A user's in-game persona can buy and furnish a house, plot land, or run a virtual store. Owners of virtual property may enjoy additional benefits, such as invitations to private gatherings or access to otherwise inaccessible parts of the Metaverse.

The principles of virtual property and ownership are foundational to the Metaverse because they give users a feeling of control over their virtual possessions. This provides users with a sense of control and direction in the Metaverse and stimulates virtual economies.

Digital Currencies and Economies

Because they make it possible for people to engage in commerce and trade in virtual spaces, digital currencies and economies are a central notion of the Metaverse. Using digital currencies, users can purchase and sell virtual goods and services and participate in other economic activities in the Metaverse.

Currency in the Metaverse can take many forms, from the platform and virtual-world-specific tokens to more universal cryptocurrencies like Bitcoin or Ethereum. The value of these virtual currencies can be traded for fiat money or even real-world goods and services.

Numerous varieties of virtual economies and currencies exist in the Metaverse. In some virtual environments, players can acquire virtual goods and services to sell to other players or complete missions and earn virtual currency. In some cases, users may be able to buy virtual currency with real money or trade it for other digital currencies.

Because they facilitate economic activity and exchange between users in the Metaverse, digital currencies and economies are a crucial pillar concept. In addition, they enable the establishment and growth of industries and commercial ventures in the Metaverse, which may or may not have some connection to the real-world economy.

Governance and Regulation

As guiding principles for the administration of virtual spaces, governance and regulation are essential pillars of the Metaverse. Community-based methods, self-regulation by virtual world operators, and external regulation by governments or other authorities are all viable options for establishing order and safety.

Community-based governance is a popular method of Metaverse administration, in which virtual world users have a say in policymaking and establishing community standards. Voting systems, forums, and other types of democratic engagement all play a role in fostering this style of leadership.

Self-regulation by virtual world operators is another kind of metaverse governance. Virtual world administrators create and implement policies that govern player behavior in this framework. Examples include taking precautions to safeguard users, guarding intellectual property, and forestalling fraud or abuse.

There is also the possibility of government or other non-internal regulation of the Metaverse. Compliance with data privacy, intellectual property, and consumer protection laws and regulations may necessitate this sort of regulation.

The stability and integrity of virtual environments rely on governance and regulation, two important anchoring concepts of the Metaverse. They safeguard the interests of metaverse users and businesses and can influence the direction the Metaverse takes in the future.

Different Forms of the Metaverse

How one accesses the Metaverse can cause it to take on several distinct appearances. These appearances are determined by the technology and gadgets employed. The following are some of the primary manifestations of the Metaverse:

The Metaverse of Virtual Reality (VR)

A virtual reality (VR) metaverse is an entirely immersive digital environment, and people can enter it using VR headsets or other devices. When a person puts on a virtual reality headset, all sensations are immediately transported to the virtual world. They communicate with the environment and other users by hand gestures or controllers. Simulations of gaming, teaching, and training are typical applications for virtual reality (VR) metaverses.

The capacity of VR metaverses to wholly submerge the user in a digital setting is among the most significant advantages offered by these environments. This may be especially helpful for activities like gaming, in which the user can have a comprehensive experience of and interact with a virtual world. Virtual reality (VR) metaverses can also be used for educational and training simulations, allowing users to acquire new abilities or practice processes in a safe and controlled setting.

A variety of virtual reality headsets are available on the market today, including standalone VR headsets that can function independently of a computer or smartphone and PC-based VR headsets that must be used in conjunction with a computer to function. VR metaverses are also possible through VR-enabled mobile devices like smartphones and tablets.

The virtual reality (VR) industry has seen significant advancements in recent years, particularly regarding resolution, the field of view, and tracking accuracy. However, there are still obstacles to conquer to deliver a virtual reality experience that is wholly immersive and operates without a hitch. These challenges include motion sickness, latency, and the requirement that enormous volumes of data be delivered in real-time. As virtual reality technology advances, we anticipate seeing more applications and use cases in a broad range of businesses.

The Metaverse of Augmented Reality (AR) Technology

A digital environment superimposed on top of the natural world is called an augmented reality metaverse (AR metaverse). AR glasses or devices that show digital content in the user's field of view are required to access the AR metaverse. AR metaverses can improve activities in the real world, such as shopping, gaming, or tourism, by adding additional levels of information and interactivity provided by digital platforms.

The capacity to enhance the physical world with digital information is one of the most significant advantages offered by AR metaverses. For instance, augmented reality glasses may be used to display information about restaurants or monuments in the immediate area, or they could be used to provide step-by-step directions for performing a specific task. AR metaverses can also be used for entertainment, such as giving players immersive and interactive gaming experiences in the real world.

Many augmented reality (AR) devices such as AR glasses, contact lenses, AR-enabled smartphones, and tablets, can be purchased today. Some augmented reality devices utilize a camera to take a picture of the user's surroundings in the real world and superimpose digital information on top of that picture. Other AR devices use transparent displays to place the digital information right in the user's line of sight.

The application of augmented reality (AR) technology can bring about a revolution in various fields, including retail, advertising, education, and the entertainment industry. However, many obstacles need to be conquered before a natural and seamless augmented reality experience can be provided. These problems include the inaccuracy of tracking, the delay that results from it, and the requirement for robust networks and servers that can handle real-time interactions. We anticipate seeing a growing number of applications and use cases for augmented reality technology across a wide range of sectors as the technology continues to advance.

The Metaverse of Mixed Reality (MR)

The virtual and real worlds come together in perfect harmony in a mixed reality (MR) Metaverse, which is a combination of virtual reality (VR) and augmented reality (AR). Users can interact simultaneously with virtual and actual environments using MR headsets or smart glasses. Because they enable users to engage with virtual and physical items in real-time, MR Metaverses can transform many industries, including manufacturing, design, and education.

The immersive qualities of virtual reality (VR) are combined with the ground-level integration of augmented reality (AR) in MR Metaverses. Users can interact with virtual items as if they were physically present in the real world, and vice versa. This is made possible by the usage of augmented reality. A user, for instance, may use MR gloves to manipulate a virtual object as if it were a real thing, or they could use MR glasses to see virtual objects shown in their physical environment. Both of these examples include the usage of mixed reality technology.

However, even though MR devices are still in the early phases of research, they have the potential to change a wide variety of industries. For instance, MR could be utilized in the manufacturing industry to assist with assembly and maintenance duties and for designing and testing prototypes in a virtual environment before their physical construction. In the field of design, MR might be used to visualize and interact with 3D models in real time, which would allow for design workflows that are both more efficient and accurate. MR has the potential to be utilized in the field of education to improve the overall quality of the learning experience for students by bringing virtual objects and experiences into the classroom.

Achieving a high level of realism and accuracy in virtual objects and environments is a primary obstacles that must be overcome while working with MR. This necessitates the utilization of cutting-edge tracking and visualization technologies, in addition to dependable networks and servers that can handle real-time interactions. We anticipate increasing applications and use cases in various sectors as MR technology develops and matures.

Virtual Worlds

Users can often engage with one another and the environment in real-time within virtual worlds since they are digital environments that may be accessed through a computer or another device. Because they are virtual shared spaces that can be accessed through the internet and produced by the confluence of virtually improved physical reality and physically persistent virtual space, they can be regarded as part of the Metaverse.

Virtual worlds typically include a high level of immersion, which means that users have the sensation that they are actually "within" the environment and can experience a powerful sense of presence.

The term "virtual worlds" refers to an umbrella term that encompasses a diverse range of online communities. These can be as basic as online discussion boards and chat rooms or as intricate and intricate as landscapes that imitate real-world locations or construct new worlds. While some virtual worlds are intended to be social gathering places, others emphasize adventuring and finding new things.

Avatars are digital representations of people that can be used to interact with the environment in which they are located and with other users. Users of many different virtual worlds can create and personalize their avatars. Personalization of avatars is possible in several ways, including altering their physical look, attire, and accessories.

It is also possible for virtual worlds to have economies in which users can earn and spend virtual currency and exchange virtual products and services with one another. Because of this, creating virtual economies and even real-world economic effects are possible as some virtual goods and services can be procured and sold using currency from the real world.

Virtual worlds provide users with a novel and immersive form of the Metaverse that enables them to engage with one another and with digital settings in various ways. They can completely transform how we think about and engage with the digital world.

Online Games

Because they are digital environments that can be accessed through the internet and allow users to interact with one another and with the environment in real-time, online games can be considered a form of the Metaverse. Online games, much like other types in the Metaverse, typically feature a high degree of immersion, which means that players get the sensation that they are actually "inside" the scene and can experience a powerful sense of presence.

Users of an online game can earn and spend their unique virtual currency and exchange virtual products and services with one another. Online games can also have their unique virtual economies. Because of this, they are creating virtual economies, and even real-world economic effects are possible. Some virtual goods and services can be bought and sold using currency from the real world.

Social features are commonly available in online games, enabling players to communicate and come together to establish communities. The immersive quality of the Metaverse can also be enhanced by the presence of virtual worlds or environments that players can investigate and engage with.

Users are given the ability to play and compete. They communicate with other people from any location in the world through online games, making this type of Metaverse important and also relatively popular. They can bring people together while also providing a gaming experience that is one-of-a-kind and immersive.

Peeking Into the Metaverse Economy

The term "Metaverse Economy" describes the financial transactions that occur in a virtual reality environment or another fully immersive internet environment. The potential for the Metaverse to significantly contribute to global GDP rises with its expansion and development.

The current economic climate in the metaverse

Even though the metaverse economy is just starting, it's expanding and proliferating. Digi-Capital predicts that by 2025, the Metaverse economy will be worth $3.2 trillion. Several factors such as the popularity of online games and e-sports, the proliferation of virtual social spaces, and the expansion of virtual reality, are driving this.

Growth and development potential

The future prosperity of the Metaverse Economy is bright. The Metaverse will undoubtedly grow more integral to our daily lives as more and more people learn to appreciate the advantages of virtual and immersive online settings. This can foster the expansion of current enterprises that have adopted virtual reality technology and the emergence of new industries and business models within the Metaverse.

The metaverse economy: threats and possibilities

As the economy of the Metaverse develops, it will encounter several difficulties and possibilities. Clear and consistent rules and laws governing behavior in the Metaverse must be established. This is necessary to avoid fraud and abuse in the Metaverse and keep it a welcoming and safe space for all users. Moreover, innovative payment and transaction mechanisms must satisfy the Metaverse economy's specific needs. This will become increasingly crucial as more individuals utilize virtual currencies and conduct virtual transactions within the Metaverse.

The Metaverse economy also offers several advantages. As an illustration, the Metaverse may present novel approaches for companies to connect and interact with their target audiences and fresh markets in which entrepreneurs and inventors can introduce and market their wares. Virtual events, conferences, and other forms of gatherings could be hosted in the Metaverse, engendering critical monetary benefits.

The perspective of the economics of the metaverse

Though its precise trajectory into the future remains unclear, the Metaverse economy undoubtedly has the potential to grow into a significant player in the global economy. As more and more individuals realize the benefits of virtual and immersive online settings, the Metaverse will expand and develop in intriguing new ways.

Key takeaways

To sum up, this chapter "What is the Metaverse?" has presented the following significant points:

- A shared, persistent virtual area where users can engage in real-time interaction with one another and with virtual items is known as the Metaverse. Realities like VR, AR, and MR are all types of this technology.
- Immersion, presence, and agency are the pillars of the Metaverse, allowing users to feel as though they are truly present in a virtual world.
- Since virtual goods and services, virtual real estate, and the monetization of user-generated content are all on the rise in the Metaverse, this might have a profound effect on the global economy.
- The Metaverse is a fascinating and developing area with the potential to radically alter how we communicate with one another and the wider world.

2

HOW TO INVEST IN METAVERSE?

Numerous industry professionals believe that the Metaverse will constitute a sizeable portion of the world's overall economy in the not-too-distant future, making it a potentially lucrative investment option. The Metaverse provides access to a diverse selection of investment alternatives, including virtual goods, non-fungible tokens (NFTs), cryptocurrencies, stocks, and real estate.

The continued expansion and development of the Metaverse offer a one-of-a-kind chance for investors to join in on the ground floor and enjoy the profits as it becomes more widespread and continues to grow. It is anticipated that the Metaverse will significantly influence gaming, entertainment, and e-commerce as it provides individuals with a fresh and engaging new method to communicate with one another, entertain themselves, and conduct business.

Investing in the Metaverse could be risky because of how new and rapidly evolving it is. However, the potential profits could be enormous for individuals ready to take risks and participate in the market early. Before investing in the Metaverse, it is essential to conduct extensive research and thoroughly understand the risks and potential rewards. Additionally, it is critical to remain current on the most recent developments and trends to make informed investment decisions.

Can You Invest in the Metaverse?

You can put money into the Metaverse. However, the Metaverse is not a single digital universe; instead, numerous metaverses can be discovered. For instance, two of the most well-known platforms in cryptocurrencies are now Decentraland (CRYPTO: MANA) and The Sandbox (CRYPTO: SAND). Mana and Sand are the "native" currencies of their respective metaverse platforms, enabling users to do things like buying virtual real estate. The tokens' value can go up if more people use the platforms they are used on.

On the other hand, investing in metaverse cryptocurrencies can be difficult because predicting which platform would ultimately be the most adopted one will take time and effort. Because there is a difference between each one, one must conduct extensive research before investing.

Improving user metrics does not automatically increase the value of metaverse tokens, in any case. According to DappRadar, the price of Mana tokens went down by more than 80% between November 2021 and June 2022, even though user metrics were reasonably consistent during this period.

The risk associated with investing in Metaverse coins might be relatively high. The same is true for tokens that cannot be converted into cash (NFTs). NFTs represent digital ownership of assets such as photographs, music, and tickets, among other things. It is challenging to forecast whether or not possessing digital property within a Metaverse platform will be cost-effective at some point in the future.

It is likely in the best interests of investors to focus more on the real-world enterprises that are establishing and making money from the trend of the Metaverse.

Metaverse Categories to Invest

Those who make frequent cryptocurrency purchases will have direct experience of the metaverse expansion over the past year, with several projects contributing to introducing this idea to the general public.

The following five strategies will detail how to invest in the Metaverse effectively; each strategy comes with its own set of distinct advantages for investors:

- Metaverse Games
- Metaverse NFTs
- Metaverse Crypto
- Metaverse Real Estate
- Metaverse Stocks

Let's take a deeper look at the strategies outlined up top by explaining what they are and how they can benefit investors over a more extended period.

Metaverse Games

Our recommendation for the most effective approach to investing in the Metaverse is to do so through either the top metaverse NFT projects or metaverse gaming. This game subgenre has experienced meteoric expansion over the past year, spurred mainly by high-profile initiatives such as Decentraland and The Sandbox. Despite this, there is a steady stream of launches of smaller projects that aim to profit from the achievements of those that came before them.

Metaverse games are precisely what their name implies: they are gaming platforms within the Metaverse. The fact that many of the best coins in the Metaverse are native to these gaming projects makes it possible for them to function faultlessly. The degree of immersion that video games can provide for players makes them enticing to gamers.

Those who have seen the film "Ready Player One" by Steven Spielberg will have a solid understanding of the appearance of Metaverse games. They provide gamers with access to detailed 3D environments in which they may build their avatars and interact with other players' avatars. This presents a new way to interact with other people, a method likely to become even more widespread in the world we live in after the pandemic.

"Play-to-earn" (P2E) methods are one of the most tempting elements for gamers, and some of the most undervalued cryptocurrencies are involved in the metaverse gaming niche. Thanks to these mechanisms, players can receive incentives (in the form of Bitcoin) for their activities while playing the game. Players now have the opportunity to earn real money through their gaming talent.

One of the game projects in the Metaverse that has recently garnered notice from the media is called Battle Infinity. This innovative project integrates a fantasy sports league into its Metaverse, allowing sports lovers to engage in competitive gameplay and earn rewards based on their level of expertise. IBAT, exclusive to Battle Infinity, is the currency used to pay these incentives.

Many investors are considering purchasing Battle Infinity to acquire exposure to the project's expansion because it possesses many other appealing aspects. Battle Store is one of them, enabling users to participate in various multiplayer pay-to-win games while increasing the potential for rewards. The Battle Infinity Telegram group is the place for individuals curious about gaining additional information regarding this exciting project.

Top 5 Metaverse games:

- Battle Infinity
- Decentraland
- The Sandbox
- Axie Infinity
- Gods Unchained

Metaverse NFTs

Investing in the Metaverse through NFTs is yet another common practice. In the past year, many of the most successful non-fungible tokens (NFTs) have been part of metaverse-based initiatives because of their valuable qualities. The ability of non-fungible tokens (NFTs) to enable "real" ownership of in-game assets is a primary selling points of these tokens from the Metaverse perspective.

In the Gods Unchained game, for instance, the in-game playing cards have the structure of non-fungible tokens (NFTs). This ensures that all of a player's cards are legitimately theirs, making it impossible for anyone to steal or change them in any way. Consequently, the idea of hacking or cheating within the game needs to be improved (or eliminated) entirely.

If items in the game are arranged as NFTs, an additional benefit is that they are more easily tradable. Battle Infinity, described above, is currently one of the most exciting NFT projects available and provides this feature. Players can purchase, sell, and trade in-game items through Battle Market, a specialized NFT marketplace part of the Battle Infinity ecosystem. Battle Market is also known as Battle Market.

IBAT, Battle Infinity's native token, can be used by users, for instance, to make purchases at the Battle Market and update the appearance of their in-world avatar with new clothing. Since supply and demand tend to be the primary elements that determine the price of each NFT. This provides an additional choice for the best way to invest in the Metaverse. Therefore, as the number of people who use the platform increases, NFTs will inevitably become harder to come by and more valuable.

The finest non-flip-to-win (NFT) games, such as Battle Infinity, allow players to buy non-flippable pieces of virtual land within the game's setting. These non-flippable plots of land are structured as NFTs. This idea will be discussed in greater depth later in the guide; nonetheless, you must be aware of it as it emphasizes the ongoing significance of NFTs inside the Metaverse.

Top 5 Metaverse NFTs

- Battle Infinity
- Lucky Block
- Gods Unchained
- Decentraland
- Axie Infinity

Metaverse Crypto

Investing in the Metaverse through its native cryptocurrency is another viable option. In a word, native tokens of metaverse-based enterprises are meant to be called "metaverse crypto." Tokens like this are typically used for various purposes, including transactions, staking, and governance. Let's take a closer look.

- **In-world transactions:** The native token of a given Metaverse is typically accepted as payment for goods purchased from the respective in-world marketplace. Users have the option, for instance, of purchasing Axie Infinity and then employing tokens to acquire extra Axies for usage within the game. This implies that sellers are paid in Metaverse crypto, which can be converted into another digital currency.
- **Staking:** Staking in crypto currency involves "freezing" tokens for a predetermined time, typically contributing to the platform's increased security level. Many Metaverse platforms have their staking mechanisms, enabling token holders to create a yield on their holdings while benefiting the larger ecosystem. These mechanisms are offered to users to attract more users to the platform.
- **Governance:** many initiatives that make up the Metaverse are organized as a decentralized autonomous organization or DAO. The individuals who own tokens govern the platform. Most successful cryptocurrency DAO initiatives allow token holders to vote on governance proposals, and the proposals that receive the maximum number of votes are implemented.

The list just presented needs to be more comprehensive because there are so many different applications for Metaverse cryptocurrencies. They also make investing in the Metaverse simple, as they are frequently listed on the most reputable cryptocurrency exchanges at this time. Therefore, even investors who aren't actively participating in a particular Metaverse can acquire exposure to its growth by purchasing tokens.

Axie Infinity is an excellent illustration, as the value of AXS tokens had increased to approximately $164 by November 2021. Earlier in the year, when the value of MANA tokens increased by more than 110%, investors who had decided to purchase Decentraland were handsomely rewarded. Those interested in investing in the Metaverse can buy IBAT tokens during the presale phase of Battle Infinity's ICO to obtain exposure to the project's expansion in the weeks and months.

Top 5 Metaverse cryptocurrencies:

- Axie Infinity
- Ethereum
- Decentraland
- Battle Infinity
- Enjin

Metaverse Real Estate

As a result of its one-of-a-kind approach to property ownership and leasing, Metaverse real estate has emerged as one of the fascinating aspects of this expanding industry. Those interested in learning how to invest in Metaverse real estate can participate in projects allowing users to buy virtual land parcels.

Since its 3D globe contains over 90,000 plots of land measuring 16 meters by 16 meters, Decentraland is one of the most notable projects that provide this feature (called LAND). LAND is a non-fungible token (NFT) that can be acquired with either MANA, Decentraland's native currency, or Ethereum.

Because of where they are situated relative to other parcels of property, some areas of land are considered to have a higher market value than others. Some of the land parcels close to the

Genesis Plaza in Decentraland were estimated to be worth more than $13,000 in 2021. The fact that these plots are merely 16 meters by 16 meters demonstrates that real estate in the Metaverse can be expensive under certain conditions.

A report published by CNBC states that the value of virtual land transactions in the Metaverse surpassed $500 million in 2021. The potential benefits of virtual property ownership to investors were a significant factor. Not only can investors profit from an increase in the property's worth as a result of the growing popularity of the project, but they can also create returns by renting out the property.

Renting works precisely as one might imagine, enabling owners of virtual land to lease their property to other users in exchange for payment. The Battle Arena feature of Battle Infinity incorporates this technique, allowing users to rent land from one another and then use that land for advertising purposes. This is made possible through virtual billboards, for which payment can be made in IBAT.

Because this "land" is still only a collection of pixels contained within a 3D reality, people interested in learning how to invest in Metaverse real estate must, in the end, make sure the land they buy has some value that cannot be replicated. Nevertheless, as demonstrated by various NFT land projects, it is possible to generate a profit from astute investments in this market.

Top 5 Metaverse real estate projects:

- Decentraland
- Battle Infinity
- The Sandbox
- Somnium Space
- Meta Mansions

Metaverse Stocks

The topic of metaverse stocks brings the conversation about the most fruitful ways to invest in the Metaverse to a close. There are many opportunities to invest in Metaverse equities, which will appeal to investors who would rather transact business in the equity market than the cryptocurrency market.

It's possible that the best equities for the Metaverse don't offer "direct" exposure to the expansion of a particular platform but to the expansion of the sector as a whole. One excellent illustration of this is the company known as Meta Platforms, formerly Facebook, now heavily involved in virtual reality (VR) and advancing concepts related to the Metaverse.

When searching for enterprises to invest in the Metaverse, it is simple to diversify a portfolio and avoid being "overexposed" to a single type of project. Since the chips manufactured by Nvidia are currently used to power various metaverse initiatives, the company is a popular choice. Naturally, if the Metaverse grows and more projects use Nvidia's chips, the company's bottom line and share price will benefit from this development, which will be positive for both.

Many well-established companies are eager to experiment with ideas linked to virtual worlds, and many are active in the Metaverse, home to some of the most inexpensive stocks. Because it has formed strategic alliances with companies like Decentraland and Roblox to bolster its presence in the Metaverse, Nike has emerged as a leader among the equities of the Metaverse that are now available for investment.

Investing in Metaverse equities is a fantastic strategy to acquire direct exposure to the expansion of the business while also providing indirect exposure to a particular project. Additionally, the process of buying stocks is typically more user-friendly than the process of buying cryptocurrency; hence, this strategy may be better suited to individuals who are new to the market.

Top 5 Metaverse stocks:

- Meta Platforms
- Nvidia
- Nike
- Coinbase
- Roblox

Primary Ways to Invest in Metaverse

Direct and indirect investment are the two most common approaches to the Metaverse's financial markets. The term "direct investment in the metaverse" refers to directly purchasing virtual assets or property within the context of a virtual world. Buying virtual real estate, such as virtual land or property, or virtual goods, such as clothing or accessories for avatars are two examples of what this can entail. Buying virtual real estate or virtual commodities can be done simultaneously (digital representations of users in the virtual world). Users of certain virtual worlds can produce virtual goods and services, which they can then sell to other users.

Putting money into businesses or innovations in some way connected to the Metaverse is what is meant by "indirect investment" in the Metaverse. Investing in companies that create technologies for virtual reality (VR) or augmented reality (AR) and investing in organizations that operate virtual worlds or offer virtual goods or services are examples of this type of activity.

Investing directly in the Metaverse can be done in a few different ways:

- **Purchase a piece of a virtual estate:** Users of certain virtual worlds, such as Second Life and Decentraland can acquire digital land. This may

comprise a piece of virtual land, a virtual building, or another type of structure.
- **Purchase virtual goods:** Many virtual worlds feature in-game economies that enable players to buy, sell, and trade virtual products. This may include clothing, accessories, and other goods for virtual avatars.
- **Some virtual worlds allow players to make and sell their original virtual goods and services:** Making your unique avatar, laying out your virtual world, or providing virtual services like online tours or lessons all fall in this category.

Investing in the Metaverse can also be done in a variety of indirect ways:

- **Invest in businesses working on virtual reality or augmented reality technology:** Many companies are now developing virtual and augmented reality technologies, anticipated to play a significant part in the expansion of the Metaverse. Obtaining exposure to the development of the Metaverse can be accomplished by investing in the companies mentioned earlier.
- **Invest in businesses that run virtual worlds or provide virtual goods or services:** Some companies run virtual worlds or provide virtual goods or services, such as games or social networks. You may put your money into those businesses.
- **Invest in businesses utilizing virtual or augmented reality in their operations:** Some enterprises utilize VR or AR in their company operations for training or marketing purposes.

Obtaining exposure to the expansion of the Metaverse can be accomplished by investing in the companies mentioned earlier.

It is essential to remember that investing in the Metaverse comes with dangers, just like investing in anything else. Before making investment decisions, one must study the possible downsides and upsides.

Top Metaverse Investors

Many various types of enterprises either currently have a stake in the Metaverse or will soon, providing ample chances for indirect investors. Many corporations view the Metaverse as an important area for future growth. We've broken down the four main sectors to keep an eye on and provide examples of some of the most famous companies operating there.

Technology platforms

Tech behemoths such as Alphabet, Amazon, and Linden Labs, which developed the first immersive virtual platform Second Life, Meta, formerly known as Facebook and Microsoft are all making significant investments in developing their very own metaverse platforms. More information is provided below on the following three major technological platforms:

- **Alphabet.** The company that owns Google is investing millions of dollars into the research and development of Web 3.0, the next generation of technologies to be used for the World Wide Web and serve as the infrastructure for the Metaverse.
- **Meta.** The social media giant is responsible for the development and launch of Meta Horizon Worlds,

being marketed as a virtual, immersive social universe in which users can explore the plethora of digital worlds created by Meta developers or create their very own.
- **Microsoft.** With the launch of Azure Digital Twins, Microsoft is allowing its users to create a digital representation of real-world things, places, business processes, and people. In return, Microsoft receives valuable insights it can use to develop and improve its products and the overall customer experience.

Gaming platforms

As a result of their ability to provide players with immersive gaming experiences, gaming platforms have been at the vanguard of the Metaverse since its inception. As a result, they attracted legions of devoted fans even before the concept became mainstream. More information is provided below on the following three major gaming platforms:

- For over a decade, the gaming industry has been a focus for the company known as Activision Blizzard. It has been able to generate revenue from its platform. For instance, players of World of Warcraft use real-world currency to acquire virtual items for use within the game, such as pets and mounts. The proposed acquisition of Activision Blizzard by Microsoft for $68.7 billion is currently awaiting approval from relevant regulatory authorities.
- Roblox is an online entertainment platform that enables users to meet new people, share stories and experiences, make connections based on shared

passions, and go on digital adventures. Roblox Studio is a free set of tools the company provides developers to construct, publish, and run 3D worlds.
- WeChat's parent company, Tencent, has a stake in the gaming industry through its subsidiary, Epic Games. Tencent owns WeChat. Fortnite, one of the most renowned online video games of all time, was developed by Epic Games. Fortnite Creative is a new gaming platform that allows users to design their characters and environments within the game.

Chip manufacturers

Because of the enormous amounts of computing power needed to support immersive digital experiences, it is generally accepted that chipmakers benefit from the metaverse development. Specifically, this belief is based on which manufacturers of semiconductors will emerge victorious remains to be seen. The following are two companies making significant investments in bringing online experiences to life:

- Nvidia is investing significantly in the Metaverse, using its flagship product, Nvidia Omniverse. Nvidia Omniverse is a platform that enables real-time acceleration of complex 3D workflows and new ways to visualize, simulate, and code.
- At the beginning of 2022, Qualcomm established a Metaverse fund of one hundred million dollars to target strategic investments in mixed-reality companies and developers. It plans to become the industry standard bearer regarding Metaverse hardware for immersive experiences like virtual

reality headsets, augmented reality glasses, and holographic projectors.

Software

What elements are required to represent a structure such as a theater or a concert hall? Here are two companies that are fully committed to the process of developing the necessary software for the Metaverse.

- Autodesk is a company that offers software and services for 3D design, engineering, and entertainment. Platforms for virtual, augmented, and extended reality has been included in the company's foray into the Metaverse. These platforms include Civil 3D, Fusion 360, Maya, and 3ds, Max. The value proposition is to make it possible for customers to create digital twins and run simulations efficiently and cost-effective.
- Unity Software initially developed software for video games; however, it is now a company that runs an interactive 3D content platform that invests heavily in the Metaverse. This year, it struck a relationship with Insomniac Events, the leading live music experience development firm, to give its fan base access to a persistent metaverse world in which they may virtually engage in live music events.

Finally, the Metaverse offers a lucrative investment opportunity for those ready to take risks and get in early. Investing in the Metaverse can be done in many different ways, including purchasing assets to hold, trading on exchanges, taking part in initial coin offerings (ICOs) or initial exchange offerings (IEOs), or funding businesses working on Metaverse-related technology or applications. Investing in the Metaverse can yield substantial returns, but only if you do your homework and fully grasp the associated risks and benefits.

Key takeaways

Since the Metaverse is still a young and rapidly developing industry, it is crucial to keep abreast of the most recent advancements and trends before committing capital there. The most important ideas presented in this chapter are:

- There are many different types of assets available for purchase in the Metaverse.
- Investing in the Metaverse can be done in various ways such as purchasing and keeping assets, trading on exchanges, taking part in initial coin offerings (ICOs), or funding businesses creating Metaverse technology or applications.
- Before making any financial commitments, you must do your homework to fully understand the dangers and potential rewards of investing in the Metaverse.
- Because of the quick pace of change in the Metaverse, investors must keep abreast of the field's most recent innovations and trends.

3

OPPORTUNITIES AND RISKS OF METAVERSE

This chapter's objectives are to delve into the advantages and disadvantages afforded by the Metaverse, debunk some of the more widespread misconceptions concerning the technology, investigate the economic impact of the Metaverse, discuss some of the lucrative career opportunities available in the field, and think about the possibility of an open metaverse.

Even though the Metaverse is still in its infancy, it has the potential to change many different industries and parts of society. These industries and aspects include social connections, entertainment, education, tourism, and commerce. However, just like any other brand-new piece of technology, the Metaverse comes with its unique set of problems and potential dangers, all of which must be carefully evaluated and dealt with in some way.

We will discuss the numerous opportunities and threats made possible by the Metaverse in contrast to the myths and misunderstandings surrounding it. In addition, we will investigate the economic effects of the Metaverse and the employment opportunities it creates. We will also explore the idea of an open metaverse and its potential benefits and drawbacks.

Opportunities Enable by the Metaverse

The Metaverse, also known as the virtual reality sphere, provides users with many options to engage in novel and fascinating forms of experience and interaction with the outside world. The following is a list of opportunities made possible by the Metaverse:

- Simulations and virtual reality experiences: The Metaverse allows people to experience and take part in immersive virtual reality environments that mimic or simulate situations that occur in the real world. This can encompass anything from simulated training programs for the military or emergency responders to virtual theme parks and adventures, virtual tours of historical or cultural places, and even virtual tours of theme parks and adventures. The Metaverse functions as a platform that allows users to create their own unique virtual reality experiences and share them with other users. The potential uses are extensive.
- The Metaverse allows users to purchase, sell, and trade virtual real estate and assets and perform business transactions within virtual surroundings. In addition, the Metaverse enables users to engage in commercial activities. Users can buy virtual property or buildings or manufacture and sell virtual goods and services in a virtual environment. The Metaverse paves the way for new possibilities in advertising and marketing because businesses can now construct virtual

experiences and surroundings to exhibit their goods and services.

- Thanks to the Metaverse, people can now participate in virtual events and entertainment. These events and entertainment can be concerts, festivals, sporting events, and many other types of gatherings. These gatherings may occur in simulated settings that are exact copies of real-world locations or entirely made-up universes. People can also develop and host their own virtual events and entertainment thanks to the Metaverse, which offers a new platform for artists, entertainers, and other creators to communicate and interact with the viewers of their work.

- Education and training in a virtual environment: The Metaverse presents new options for education and training since it enables individuals to acquire knowledge and hone their abilities within virtual environments that accurately represent the actual world. This can encompass various activities such as simulated fieldwork or laboratory experiments, online classes, and virtual classrooms. The Metaverse provides a platform for educators and trainers, allowing them to reach students and trainees in new ways and engage with them in other ways.

- Collaboration and communication in virtual settings: The Metaverse makes it possible for individuals to collaborate and interact with one another in virtual environments, regardless of where they are physically located. This can encompass various activities such as online gatherings and conferences, co-working spaces, social events, and get-togethers. The Metaverse provides a new platform for people to connect and collaborate, promoting increased levels of communication and collaboration.

Risks Enabled by the Metaverse

The Metaverse presents its users with many exciting prospects; nevertheless, it also shows them various hazards and possible adverse outcomes. Users are put in a position where they could be put in harm's way by several risks, some of which are mentioned below:

- Privacy and safety issues arise as a result of the fact that the Metaverse requires the collecting, storage, and utilization of individuals' data and information, raising privacy and safety issues. This includes the possibility of data breaches, loss of identity, and other forms of cybercrime. It is necessary for people who utilize the Metaverse to be aware of the risks that could occur and take proactive steps to protect the confidentiality of their data and personal information.
- Because of the immersive quality of the Metaverse and the capacity to participate in virtual activities for extended periods, users risk developing addiction and social isolation due to their use of virtual environments. People have the potential to get so immersed in their virtual experiences that they neglect their real-world and social lives, which can harm their overall health and well-being. It is critical for individuals to be aware of the potential for addiction and find a way to maintain a healthy equilibrium between their lives in the physical world and their lives online.

- Inequality and exclusivity in economic opportunities: The Metaverse may produce inequality and exclusivity in economic opportunities because access to virtual experiences and assets may be restricted due to financial or technological obstacles. The gap between those who can afford or have access to the Metaverse and those who cannot will widen, exacerbating the already present inequalities. All people must be able to participate in the Metaverse, ensuring participation is open to all, and efforts should be made to eliminate economic inequality.
- Disputes about intellectual property can arise because the Metaverse necessitates the production, utilization, and dissemination of many forms of virtual information and assets. This involves disagreements on ownership and control of virtual assets and concerns around infringement of copyright and trademarks. The Metaverse needs to have intellectual property rules and practices that are transparent and equitable to address these concerns.
- Ethical and moral dilemmas: The advent of the Metaverse has ushered in a new era of ethical and moral problems, particularly to the utilization of virtual surroundings and experiences. This encompasses concerns of duty and accountability for actions carried out within the Metaverse and the possibility that virtual persons or entities could be harmed or made to suffer due to these actions. The Metaverse needs to address and consider these ethical and moral problems to construct a responsible virtual reality area that can exist for an extended period.

Dispelling Metaverse Myths

The Metaverse is the subject of many myths and false beliefs, which can result in confusion and an incorrect understanding of the possibilities and potential it possesses. The following is a summary of some common misunderstandings regarding the Metaverse that need to be cleared up:

Myth: The metaverse is just for gaming.

The Metaverse is sometimes linked to the world of video games; nevertheless, it encompasses much more than that. The term "Metaverse" refers to the expansive range of virtual environments and activities. These can include learning, entertainment, business, and other domains. It is a platform for creating and sharing virtual reality experiences that transcend the gaming realm.

Myth: The metaverse is a replacement for the real world.

The real world is not meant to be replaced by the Metaverse; instead, the Metaverse serves as a supplement to the real world. The worth and significance of the material world will never be eclipsed by the existence of the Metaverse, even though it opens up fascinating new avenues for experiencing and engaging with the universe. Even if they participate in the Metaverse, people are still responsible for interacting with the physical world and leading their lives there. This is true even if they engage in virtual reality.

Myth: The metaverse is a utopia or dystopia.

The Metaverse is neither a utopia nor a dystopia; instead, it is an intricate and multifaceted world that exists within the realm of virtual reality and can be both positive and negative simultaneously. It opens up new potential and rewards and brings unknown risks and difficulties. Because the actions and decisions of its users and producers influence the Metaverse in the same way that they shape the actual world, it is essential to work toward creating a virtual reality area that is both responsible and environmentally friendly.

Myth: You need a VR headset to access the metaverse.

Virtual reality headsets are just one way to enter the Metaverse; however, other methods are also available. Access to the Metaverse is possible via various platforms and devices, including personal computers, tablets, and mobile phones. A virtual reality headset is not required to participate in or enjoy most activities and experiences available within the Metaverse.

Myth: The metaverse will replace real-life interactions.

The Metaverse is intended to supplement real-world interactions rather than serve as a substitute for them. Even if the Metaverse makes it possible to connect and communicate with other people in new ways, it cannot replace the worth or significance of interactions that take place in person. Even if they take part in the Metaverse, people still need to maintain relationships with one another grounded in the material world through face-to-face contact. It is essential to strike a healthy balance between online and offline activities if one wishes to keep their relationships happy and meaningful.

In conclusion, it is essential to debunk the myths surrounding the Metaverse to get a more profound comprehension and appreciation for its capabilities and potential. The Metaverse as a virtual reality realm is both intricate and varied. While it presents several opportunities and advantages, it also brings about risks and difficulties. Being conscious of these risks and obstacles is crucial to building a virtual environment that is responsible, long-lasting, and accessible to people of varying abilities.

As the Metaverse continues to develop and expand, it is essential to consider the effects it will have on the economy. The Metaverse has the potential to facilitate the migration of already existing industries into the virtual world, in addition to the creation of new businesses and employment opportunities. However, it is also essential to take into account the possibility of economic disruption as well as inequality and find solutions to these problems to develop a virtual economy that is both equitable and sustainable.

Economic Impact of Metaverse

The Metaverse has the potential to have a considerable impact on the economy, not only in creating new businesses and jobs but also in facilitating the transition of already-established businesses into the digital sphere. The following are examples of the Metaverse's effects on the economy:

Possibility of the creation of new businesses and jobs

Because it provides a platform for creating and sharing virtual experiences and assets, the Metaverse presents a possibility for developing new business sectors and employment opportunities. This can involve anything from the planning and management of virtual events and the production and selling of virtual real estate to the creation and design of virtual content in virtual environments. People can also engage in new forms of trade and earn cash thanks to the Metaverse, through selling virtual products and services.

Possibility for currently operating businesses to relocate to the virtual world

Because it provides a new platform for conducting business and communicating with clients, the Metaverse allows already established business sectors to relocate to the virtual world. The Metaverse makes this option available, including everything from online storefronts and marketplaces to events and gatherings and customer assistance and service. Companies now have new ways to communicate creatively and in immersive ways with their target consumers because the Metaverse proliferates virtual worlds.

Potential for economic disruption and inequality

The economic impact of the Metaverse is not without risks and concerns since it has the potential to disrupt already existing businesses and generate economic inequality. However, despite these risks and challenges, the potential benefits are substantial. There may be a divide between those who can afford or have access to the Metaverse and those unable to participate in virtual commerce due to the possibility that financial or technological barriers may limit access to the Metaverse and the ability to participate in virtual commerce. The Metaverse needs to address and attempt to reduce the possible adverse effects of these situations and develop a virtual economy that is both just and viable.

In conclusion, the Metaverse could significantly affect the economy by spawning new businesses, providing employment opportunities in the virtual world, and facilitating the relocation of current businesses. Although the Metaverse has many potential advantages, it also has some drawbacks that must be considered, such as the possibility of economic instability and increased inequality. The Metaverse is a fluid and ever-changing environment that will affect the economy.

As the Metaverse develops, it will provide new, high-paying opportunities for those who can successfully navigate it. Virtual event planning and coordination, virtual real estate development and sales, virtual content creation and design, and other related fields are projected to be among the fastest-growing sectors in the labor market in the coming years. People now have a new opportunity to demonstrate their skills, provide value to the lives of others, and make a living thanks to the development of the Metaverse.

Lucrative Metaverse Jobs

New job opportunities will emerge within this virtual world as the Metaverse continues to grow and develop. Some of the most lucrative careers may include:

- **Virtual event planners and coordinators:** With the rise of virtual events and conferences, there will be a need for professionals who can plan and execute them in the Metaverse. This could include securing speakers and sponsors, designing the virtual event space, and managing logistics.
- **Virtual real estate developers and agents:** As the Metaverse becomes a place where people can own and develop a virtual property, professionals will need to help facilitate these transactions. This could include real estate developers who create virtual

spaces and agents who help buyers and sellers navigate the virtual property market.
- **Virtual retail and commerce specialists:** The Metaverse will also provide new opportunities for retail and commerce, with virtual stores and shopping centers being developed within the virtual world. Professionals skilled in e-commerce and digital marketing will be in high demand to help businesses succeed in the new environment.
- **Virtual education and training instructors:** The Metaverse could also become a popular place for education and training, with virtual classrooms and training sessions being held in the virtual world. Educators and trainers skilled at creating engaging and interactive learning experiences will be highly demanded to lead these sessions.
- **Virtual entertainment and gaming designers and developers:** The Metaverse will also be a place for entertainment and gaming, with a wide range of virtual experiences being developed. Professionals with skills in game design and development, as well as those skilled in creating immersive and interactive virtual experiences, will be in high demand.
- **Virtual healthcare professionals:** The Metaverse could also provide new opportunities for healthcare professionals, with virtual consultations and therapy sessions being held in the virtual world. This could include virtual visits with doctors and nurses, to virtual mental health counseling sessions.
- **Virtual social media and community managers:** As the Metaverse becomes a place for socializing and networking, professionals will need to manage and grow virtual communities. This could include social

> media managers skilled at creating and promoting content and community managers who facilitate discussions and engagement.

In summary, there is a vast selection of well-paying and exciting work in the Metaverse. Professionals in various sectors can benefit from the Metaverse, from event organizers and real estate brokers to educators, trainers, game designers, doctors, social media, and community managers.

Interoperability and open standards will significantly affect how work will be done in the Metaverse as it grows and changes. A Metaverse with open standards and decentralized governance could create a level playing field for everyone, including individuals and businesses. As developers and producers work together to make new virtual experiences and improve the ones we already have, this could foster a culture of working together and being creative. As the Metaverse grows, it will be interesting to see what kinds of jobs and ways to make a living come up in a dynamic virtual world that is changing rapidly.

Open Metaverse

An open metaverse refers to a virtual world constructed on open standards and interoperability. This type of virtual world makes it possible for various virtual experiences and platforms to integrate easily with one another and collaborate on projects. An open Metaverse would also be decentralized, meaning that no one entity would have complete power over the virtual world. Instead, it would be administered by a decentralized network of individuals and organizations that collaborate to keep the virtual world running smoothly and make improvements to it.

An open metaverse has several significant advantages, including the following:

- The significance of open standards and the capacity to communicate with one another: The Metaverse can clear the problems of vendor lock-in and fragmentation that have plagued other industries thanks to the adoption of open standards. This would make it possible for various virtual experiences and platforms to effortlessly interface with one another and collaborate, resulting in a virtual world that is more unified and consistent.
- The possibility of distributed forms of administration and ownership: A decentralized metaverse is not controlled by a single entity but rather by the community of people and organizations that use it. This community would own and administer the Metaverse. This could lead to decision-making processes that are more democratic and inclusive, while also making it possible for a wider variety of people's perspectives to be heard and represented.
- An open metaverse encourages a culture of open-source development and cooperation as developers and creators work together to construct and improve virtual experiences. This may be a possibility if the Metaverse is open to the public. This could lead to faster innovation and advancement inside the Metaverse and lower entrance hurdles for new creators and developers.

In general, an open metaverse has the potential to build a virtual world that is more integrated and welcoming to people of diverse backgrounds, one in which individuals and organizations may efficiently work together and develop new ideas. It will be crucial to evaluate the role that open standards and decentralized governance can play in molding this dynamic and rapidly-evolving virtual environment as the Metaverse continues to broaden and evolve.

Key takeaways

In conclusion, here are the most important things to remember about the benefits and dangers of the Metaverse:

- Opportunities for virtual tourism, events, conferences, real estate, retail, education, training, entertainment, gaming, healthcare, therapy, socializing, and networking may be found in the Metaverse.
- The Metaverse is not without its dangers, including data breaches and identity theft, harassment and intimidation online, dependency and abuse, theft of ideas and inventions, and economic isolation.
- The Metaverse is not an alternative to the real world, a paradise or dystopia, or a location where standard rules and regulations don't apply.
- Jobs, economic growth and even the disruption or replacement of established sectors are all possibilities, thanks to the Metaverse.
- Careers in virtual event planning and coordination, virtual real estate development and brokerage, virtual retail and commerce, virtual education and training, virtual game design and development, virtual healthcare, virtual social media, and community management may all pay well in the Metaverse.
- A more coherent and welcoming virtual world might be constructed with an open metaverse based on open standards and interoperability and managed by a decentralized network of persons and organizations. As developers and producers work together to create and improve virtual experiences,

this trend will also encourage a spirit of cooperation and originality.

As this exciting and rapidly developing digital world continues to grow and develop, the Metaverse presents opportunities and threats that must be appropriately studied and controlled. By being aware of these possibilities and dangers and committing to the ideals of an open Metaverse, we can build a virtual environment that serves the interests of all parties involved and influences the course of humanity's destiny.

4

METAVERSE BUSINESS OPPORTUNITIES

The Metaverse is quickly becoming a new platform for companies to communicate with customers, exhibit their products and services, and streamline their internal operations. In this chapter, we will look into how the Metaverse can assist businesses and will likely transform the traditionally used processes in organizations. In addition, we will talk about the potential to be found in the virtual world and explore whether or not enterprises should move their operations into the Metaverse.

We will discuss some of the most successful brands in the Metaverse that are now selling digital items and then highlight potential opportunities for businesses to learn from these brands or partner with them. After reading this chapter, you will better understand the possible benefits and challenges of conducting business in the Metaverse.

How Can Metaverse Help in Business

Users can engage with each other and virtual items and environments in real-time within the Metaverse, a virtual world. It is a platform that can completely transform how companies engage with their clients and run their operations inside. The following is a list of the different ways in which businesses have the potential to gain from the Metaverse:

- **Meetings and events that are held virtually:** The Metaverse provides a platform for companies to hold virtual meetings and events in a more immersive and engaging environment. These gatherings could be conferences, trade exhibitions, product launches, or other business events. The capacity to organize and run events and meetings online is becoming an increasingly valuable skill in light of the growing prevalence of telecommuting jobs and the expanding significance of digital communication. Participants can interact with one another and the content in a way that would not be feasible with conventional video conferencing technologies - all made possible by the Metaverse.
- **Showcases of virtual goods and services:** The Metaverse allows companies to present their goods and services to potential customers in an entirely virtual environment. This can help businesses in categories like fashion, home décor, and automobile, where customers must be able to see and engage with things in person. Businesses can allow customers to explore and engage with their items in a way not feasible in the actual world by constructing virtual showrooms or stores in the Metaverse. Customers can do this in the physical world, with the potential to assist businesses in increasing sales and engaging new clients.
- **Education and training in a virtual environment:** The Metaverse can serve as a platform for delivering

training and education to the clients or workers of a company. Businesses can more quickly by developing virtual classrooms or training modules in the Metaverse. This can be especially helpful for companies that employ people from all over the world or want to broaden their customer base beyond the confines of their local market.

- **Businesses can reach new clients and grow their market presence through the metaverse, which provides a platform for doing so.** Businesses can engage with a worldwide audience and tap into new markets by establishing a presence in the Metaverse. These new markets are yet to become reachable through traditional distribution routes, and they have the likelihood to assist businesses in expanding their customer base and income.

In general, the Metaverse provides businesses with many chances to communicate with customers, demonstrate their goods and services, and improve the efficiency of their internal operations. As the Metaverse continues to mature and advance in the years to come, a growing number of businesses will likely seize the opportunities presented by its continued growth and development.

In short, the Metaverse provides several chances for companies to interact with clients, promote their wares, and improve internal operations. Businesses can take advantage of the Metaverse's unique qualities by holding virtual events and meetings, presenting items in virtual showrooms, providing training and education in virtual classrooms, while growing their client base and market reach. More and more companies will start taking advantage of the Metaverse's growth and development as it presents more opportunities.

In the following section, we will examine how the Metaverse can facilitate better teamwork and communication, expedite and simplify decision-making, and computerize and streamline company operations. Observing how the Metaverse is used to disrupt conventional business practices in the years to come should be intriguing.

Three Ways How Metaverse Will Transform Business Processes

The Metaverse is a virtual environment that provides a diverse selection of options for companies to interact with their consumers and improve the efficiency of their internal operations. The following is a list of how traditional business processes are anticipated to be transformed by the Metaverse:

1. The streamlining and computerization of specific business procedures.

The Metaverse provides platform companies can use to automate and streamline various business processes. For instance, companies can utilize the Metaverse to automate the onboarding process for new workers by allowing them to complete paperwork and training in a virtual environment. This makes the process more convenient for both the company and the employee. They also can use the Metaverse to automate the approval process for various tasks such as requests for time off or expenditure reports. Businesses can save time and resources, boost efficiency, and lower the chance of making errors when they streamline and automate the processes relevant to their operations.

2. Improving teamwork and communication for many organizations.

The Metaverse provides a medium through which individuals in different physical locations can work together and communicate in real-time. This may be especially helpful for companies that employ people from other parts of the world or rely on remote teams. Teams can share files, hold virtual meetings, and work on projects in a not-conceivable way when utilizing the available communication tools. This is all made possible by the Metaverse and helps teams work more efficiently and effectively, leading to higher production and outcomes.

3. Accelerating and improving the effectiveness of decision-making processes

Thanks to the Metaverse, businesses can make decisions faster and with better information. They can more rapidly and precisely evaluate multiple possibilities and make decisions based on real-time data if they use the Metaverse to acquire and analyze data from diverse sources. This can assist firms in making better decisions more quickly, improving efficiency and competitiveness.

The Metaverse, as a whole, possesses the potential to revolutionize conventional corporate procedures while simultaneously enhancing teamwork, communication, and decision-making. An increasing number of companies may take advantage of these capabilities as the Metaverse continues to expand and develop in the years to come.

The Metaverse has the potential to increase teamwork, communication, and decision-making over more conventional business methods. Businesses can take advantage of its unique qualities by simplifying and automating routine tasks, fostering greater cooperation and communication, and accelerating decision-making. More and more companies will use the Metaverse's features as it develops further and grows more sophisticated.

As we move forward, we will examine the many possibilities presented by the online world, such as virtual land ownership and real estate investments, virtual travel and tourism, virtual media and entertainment, and virtual shopping and apparel. It will be interesting to observe how companies use the opportunities the Metaverse presents for innovation while creating new products and services in the coming years.

Business Opportunities

The Metaverse offers a variety of opportunities for businesses to grow and innovate in the virtual space. Some potential business opportunities in the Metaverse include:

- **Virtual real estate and property establishment:** The Metaverse allows for the creation and development of virtual spaces, including offices, homes, and other properties. This will enable businesses to enter the real estate market virtually, offering virtual properties for sale or rent.
- **Virtual tourism and entertainment:** The Metaverse's immersive nature offers businesses a unique opportunity to create virtual experiences and tours that allow users to explore new places and environments. This could include virtual theme parks, historical sites, and other attractions.
- **Virtual education and training:** The ability to create and interact with virtual environments allows businesses to offer a range of educational and training experiences in the Metaverse. This could

include virtual classrooms, workshops, and other training programs.

- **Virtual health care and wellness:** The Metaverse offers the potential for remote and virtual health care, allowing patients to access medical professionals and resources from their homes. This could include virtual appointments with doctors, therapists, and other healthcare professionals and virtual wellness programs and activities.
- **Virtual concerts and immersive entertainment:** The Metaverse allows for creating virtual concerts and other types of immersive entertainment experiences. This could include virtual music festivals, theater performances, and live events.
- **Enhanced customer engagement through interactive experiences:** The Metaverse offers the opportunity for businesses to create interactive and immersive experiences for their customers. This could include virtual product demonstrations, virtual storefronts, and interactive marketing campaigns.
- **Improved learning and training through virtual environments:** The ability to create virtual training environments allows businesses to offer more engaging and interactive learning experiences for their employees. This could include virtual onboarding programs, workshops, and other training programs.
- **Branding and marketing opportunities through virtual presence:** The Metaverse offers businesses the opportunity to establish a virtual presence and create brand awareness through virtual storefronts, events, and other marketing campaigns.

- **Digital real estate for virtual storefronts and offices:** The Metaverse allows businesses to create virtual storefronts and offices, offering a cost-effective way to establish a digital presence and reach a wider audience.
- **New revenue streams through virtual experiences and services:** The Metaverse offers businesses the opportunity to create and sell virtual experiences and services, opening up new revenue streams and possibilities for growth.

In conclusion, businesses seeking virtual expansion and innovation opportunities will find wealth in the Metaverse. The Metaverse has a wide variety of business options, including virtual real estate and tourism, education and training, immersive entertainment, and customer engagement. While there are certainly risks and difficulties associated with entering the Metaverse, there are also opportunities for success and growth for forward-thinking businesses that adopt this technology early on. In the next section, we will cover the advantages of early adoption and the risks and difficulties that organizations face when entering the Metaverse.

Is Metaverse the Right Way to Go?

Businesses are considering entering the Metaverse, and there are several key considerations. When considering whether or not the Metaverse is the correct path for your company, the following are factors to take into consideration:

- **Audience:** The first thing to consider is your target audience. Are they likely to be interested in and engaged with the Metaverse? If your target audience

is not tech-savvy or interested in virtual experiences, entering the Metaverse may not be worth the investment.
- **Goals:** What are your business goals, and how will the Metaverse help you achieve them? Entering the Metaverse should align with your business objectives and help you reach your desired outcomes.
- **Resources:** Entering the Metaverse requires time, money, and other resources. Consider whether your business has the necessary resources to create a virtual presence and whether the potential returns justify the investment.
- **Competitors:** Look at your competitors and see how they use the Metaverse. Is it a competitive advantage for them and could it be for you?
- **Challenges and risks:** As with any new venture, there are potential challenges and risks to consider when entering the Metaverse. These may include technical challenges such as ensuring the stability and security of your virtual presence, as well as legal and regulatory issues, such as ensuring compliance with privacy laws.

Despite these considerations, there are also many potential benefits to early adoption of the Metaverse:

- **Increased flexibility and accessibility:** The Metaverse allows for increased flexibility and accessibility for employees and customers, enabling remote work and virtual interactions.
- **Enhanced collaboration and communication:** Virtual meetings and events in the Metaverse can

facilitate better collaboration and communication between team members, regardless of location.
- **Improved customer experiences:** The immersive and interactive nature of the Metaverse can offer enhanced customer experiences and greater engagement with your brand.
- **Cost savings:** The Metaverse can offer potential cost savings through reduced physical overhead and more efficient processes.

Overall, the decision to enter the Metaverse should be based on a thorough analysis of your business goals, audience, resources, potential challenges and risks, along with the benefits of early adoption. If the Metaverse aligns with your business objectives and offers the potential for growth and innovation, it may be a worthwhile venture to consider.

Top 12 Metaverse Brands Selling Digital Products

Several brands have emerged as leaders as the Metaverse continues to grow and evolve. These top 12 metaverse brands are notable for their innovative and successful approaches to selling digital products in the virtual world.

1. **Second Life:** Second Life is a virtual environment that enables users to create, connect, and sell digital goods. It strongly focuses on user-generated content and offers a wide range of virtual goods and services for sale, including clothing, accessories, and home decor.
2. **Roblox:** Roblox is a platform that allows users to create and play games and buy and sell virtual items. It has a large and active user base, with

millions of daily active users and billions of dollars in virtual goods sold.

3. **Minecraft:** Minecraft is a widely played sandbox computer game that allows players to construct and explore virtual worlds. It strongly focuses on user-generated content and offers a wide range of virtual goods and services for sale, including skins, textures, and mods.
4. **Fortnite:** Fortnite is a video game that features a battle royale format and has recently gained many players. It offers a range of virtual goods and services for sale, including skins, emotes, and other cosmetics.
5. **The Sims:** The Sims is a life simulation video game that allows players to create and control virtual characters and their surroundings. It strongly focuses on user-generated content and offers a wide range of virtual goods and services for sale, including clothing, accessories, and home decor.
6. **World of Warcraft:** The online role-playing game known as World of Warcraft is a type of game known as a massively multiplayer online role-playing game (MMORPG), which has a player base that is both huge and devoted. It offers a range of virtual goods and services for sale, including in-game currency, gear, and other items.
7. **Animal Crossing:** Animal Crossing is a life simulation video game that allows players to create and customize virtual towns and characters. It strongly focuses on user-generated content and offers a wide range of virtual goods and services for sale, including clothing, accessories, and home decor.

8. **Grand Theft Auto:** The video game Grand Theft Auto is an open-world action-adventure title that allows players to investigate and engage with a fictitious metropolis. It offers a range of virtual goods and services for sale, including in-game currency, vehicles, and other items.
9. **Call of Duty:** Call of Duty (popularly referred to as COD) is a popular, long-running first-person shooter video game with a vast and devoted fan base. It offers a range of virtual goods and services for sale, including in-game currency, gear, and other items.
10. **League of Legends:** League of Legends has a vast and active player community because it is a multiplayer online battle arena game. It offers a range of virtual goods and services for sale, including in-game currency, gear, and other items.
11. **Overwatch:** Overwatch is a team-based first-person shooter video game with a large and dedicated player base. It offers a range of virtual goods and services for sale, including in-game currency, gear, and other items.
12. **PUBG:** PUBG (PlayerUnknown's Battlegrounds) is a battle royale video game that has become wildly popular in recent years. It offers a range of virtual goods and services for sale, including in-game currency, gear, and other items.

These top 12 metaverse brands have established themselves as eaders in the virtual world, offering users a broad range of digital products and services. They are prime examples of the potential for success in the Metaverse for businesses looking to sell digital products. Each brand has found a unique niche and leveraged the Metaverse's immersive and interactive nature to offer engaging and innovative user experiences. These companies are well-positioned for future success and should be watched by other firms contemplating venturing into the virtual world. No doubt, the Metaverse will continue to expand and change in the coming years.

Key takeaways

Throughout this chapter, we have explored the various business opportunities the Metaverse offers for companies looking to innovate and grow in the virtual space. Some key takeaways from the chapter include

- The Metaverse can help businesses increase flexibility and accessibility, enhance collaboration and communication, improve customer experiences, and save costs.
- The Metaverse can transform business processes through virtual storefronts, virtual training and onboarding, virtual conferences and events, and virtual product demonstrations and trade shows.
- Potential business opportunities in the virtual space include virtual real estate and property development, virtual tourism and entertainment, virtual education and training, virtual health care and wellness, virtual concerts and immersive entertainment, enhanced customer engagement through interactive experiences, improved learning and training through virtual environments, branding and marketing opportunities through virtual presence, digital real estate for virtual storefronts and offices, and new revenue streams through virtual experiences and services.
- Critical considerations for businesses deciding whether the Metaverse is the right way to include audience, goals, resources, competitors, and challenges and risks.
- The potential benefits of early adoption of the Metaverse include increased flexibility and accessibility, enhanced collaboration and

communication, improved customer experiences, and cost savings.

Thanks to the Metaverse, businesses have a rare and promising chance to experiment with new ideas and expand their presence in the virtual world. The Metaverse is the next frontier for forward-thinking enterprises because of its potential to boost adaptability and accessibility, improve teamwork and communication, enrich client interactions, and cut operational expenses. It's becoming increasingly apparent that businesses with an eye on the virtual marketplace will find ample opportunity in the expanding and maturing Metaverse. The Metaverse gives companies several opportunities to interact with their customers and expand their virtual presence through virtual stores, virtual training and onboarding, virtual conferences and events, virtual product demonstrations, and trade exhibitions.

Therefore, firms interested in entering the Metaverse should assess the potential benefits of early adoption against the hurdles and hazards associated with doing so, considering factors such as their target demographic, objectives, resources, competitors, and risks. Businesses can thrive in the Metaverse and contribute to the expansion of the digital landscape by emphasizing innovation and the quality of the customer's experiences.

5

METAVERSE DEVICES AND TECHNOLOGY

The Metaverse has been presented in earlier chapters as a virtual world where users can engage in lifelike, immersive interactions with one another and with digital content. Entertainment, learning, working, and socializing are just a few fields that could see a dramatic upheaval thanks to the advent of the Metaverse.

Users require specialized hardware and software to enter and navigate the Metaverse. In this chapter, we'll go over the several metaverse devices out there, the gear you'll need to operate them, and things to consider when making your final purchase. As part of our investigation, we will examine the technologies at the heart of the Metaverse and how they interact to produce a consistent digital world. Finally, we'll go through the opportunities and threats that software developers face when designing and maintaining applications for the Metaverse, as well as the possible effects it could have on a wide range of industries, including manufacturing and transportation.

Metaverse Devices

The term "Metaverse devices" refers to specialized gear and software that allow users to access and interact with the Metaverse. Users can engage with digital content in a manner that is both realistic and immersive within the Metaverse, which is a virtual world. Users can encounter and alter digital content in the Metaverse. There are a few distinct categories of metaverse devices:

- Virtual reality headsets, also known simply as VR headsets, are head-mounted devices that immerse the user in a virtual environment by employing high-resolution displays and motion-tracking sensors. Virtual reality headsets include audio, haptic feedback, controllers for hand movements, and other types of inputs.
- AR glasses are glasses or goggles that superimpose digital content over the real world. This allows the user to observe and interact with the environment's virtual and physical parts simultaneously. Transparent screens, projection systems, or even a combination of the two may, be used in augmented reality glasses.
- Haptic devices: These devices give the user tactile feedback, such as vibrations or pressure, to increase their sense of touch while in a virtual environment. Examples of this type of feedback include: A variety of different kinds of technology, including virtual reality and augmented reality technologies, are compatible with haptic devices.

Devices for the Metaverse come with a wide range of features, capabilities, and prices. While some are more versatile and can be used for various purposes, others are explicitly tailored for specific applications, such as gaming or training. When choosing a device for the Metaverse, it is essential to consider aspects such as the amount of immersion sought, the scenario in which the device will be used, and its compatibility with other tools and systems.

Users may require additional hardware in addition to the gadget itself to properly access and interact with the Metaverse. This may contain things like controllers, microphones, external sensors, and various other types of input devices. Specific metaverse devices could need a powerful computer or mobile device and a constant internet connection to function correctly.

Things to Consider When Selecting Your Metaverse Equipment

Before you go out and buy equipment for the Metaverse, you need to consider several important factors; it should enable you to have the most enjoyable and fulfilling experience imaginable.

1. **Compatibility**: One of the first things you should do is check to see if the equipment you've selected is compatible with your computer or gaming system. This includes ensuring the device in question possesses the appropriate ports (such as HDMI and USB) and that it satisfies the system requirements for the operation of Metaverse software. If you want to use more recent metaverse technology, you should invest in a newer computer or game system if you have an older one.
2. **High-quality image and audio**: The graphics and sounds you hear and see in the Metaverse can significantly influence your overall experience. Look

for products that have screens with a high resolution as well as audio capabilities, such as three-dimensional sound. This is of utmost importance for virtual reality (VR) headsets since total immersion in the environment, both visually and aurally, is an essential component of the VR experience.
3. **Comfort and ease of use:** When using Metaverse equipment, ensure that the gadgets are simple to operate and comfortable to wear or carry for extended periods. To ensure that the equipment you purchase is comfortable, look for controls and features that are easy to understand, such as adjustable headbands or hand straps. Consider t

7 Key Technologies Powering the Metaverse

Various technologies that allow for immersive, interactive, and interconnected virtual experiences are necessary to realize the potential of the Metaverse. These technologies continuously undergo change and improvement, contributing to its continued expansion and development. The following is a list of the seven most important technologies currently being used to power the Metaverse:

1. Virtual reality (VR) is a technology that employs headgear and other equipment to create a fully immersive virtual environment that you can interact with using your senses. VR technology may be broken down into two categories: augmented and virtual. Virtual reality headsets often incorporate displays for both eyes, in-built audio and motion tracking capabilities, and sometimes even motion controllers. Virtual reality (VR) is an essential

technology for many Metaverse experiences since it enables users to immerse themselves entirely and navigate virtual environments.

2. Augmented reality (AR) is a technology that enhances a user's view of the natural world by superimposing digital information and visuals over the real environment. This technology is often accessed through a device such as a smartphone or a headset. Augmented reality (AR) in the Metaverse can produce a hybrid reality experience by superimposing virtual features on the real world. Displaying information, navigating virtual worlds, and interacting with virtual items and characters are all possible uses for augmented reality (AR).

3. 3 The creation of realistic and immersive virtual environments is made possible by the Metaverse thanks to the development of cutting-edge technologies in 3D graphics and rendering. This includes using technologies such as ray tracing and global illumination, effectively replicating how light behaves in a virtual world. Tracing how light behaves in a virtual world can be done by accurately simulating how light acts when it bounces off surfaces. Modeling, animation, shading, and rendering are significant dimensions of the graphic design industry.

4. Motion tracking and haptic feedback: Motion tracking technology, such as sensors and cameras enable the Metaverse to track and respond to the movement and activities of users. Haptic feedback refers to a user's sensation when something is touched. This can be used to control virtual avatars or objects and enable gestures and other physical interactions in the virtual world. Additionally, this

can allow physical exchanges in the real world. Haptic feedback technologies use touch and force to provide a feeling of presence and actual physical engagement within a virtual environment. This can be achieved with the use of haptic gloves, suits, or other types of wearable technology.

5. Artificial Intelligence and natural language processing: Technologies that utilize artificial intelligence (AI) and natural language processing make it possible for the Metaverse to comprehend and respond to the actions and commands of users, as well as to create and maintain virtual characters that are believable and realistic. This includes using algorithms for machine learning, which provide virtual characters the ability to adapt and react appropriately to various circumstances and learn from their interactions with people.

6. Cloud computing and distributed networks: The Metaverse depends on cloud computing and distributed networks to store and transfer data and enable users to communicate in real-time. Cloud computing enables the efficient storage and processing of large amounts of data. At the same time, distributed networks make it possible for users to access and interact with the Metaverse no matter where they are in the world. Cloud computing also makes it possible to store and process smaller amounts of data efficiently.

7. Blockchain and decentralized technologies: Using blockchain and technologies in the Metaverse can give users greater security, ownership, and control over their virtual assets and experiences. This can be beneficial for both the users and the virtual world as a whole. In addition to enabling peer-to-

peer transactions and interactions inside the Metaverse, blockchain technology allows the creation of secure and decentralized databases to store virtual assets. Decentralized technologies also make diverse Metaverse platforms and systems more interoperable and compatible.

The Metaverse is driven by various technologies that enable rich, responsive, and interconnected simulated realities. These innovations include virtual reality, augmented reality, 3D graphics and rendering, motion tracking and haptic feedback, Artificial Intelligence and natural language processing, cloud computing, distributed networks, blockchain, and decentralized technologies. These technologies will play an ever-increasing role in propelling the expansion and maturation of the Metaverse as they undergo further refinement and development.

Using the Metaverse in manufacturing for purposes such as education, prototyping, and teamwork is already changing the face of business. It also has enormous potential to improve automobile design, testing, and customer experience. We anticipate even more innovation and disruption in the years to come as more sectors adopt and incorporate metaverse technologies.

The Industrial Metaverse

Using the Metaverse in the manufacturing, construction, and other industrial sectors, is starting to alter how these businesses function. Companies can significantly enhance their levels of efficiency and productivity, as well as their financial stability, by adopting the Metaverse as a platform for training, prototyping, and collaborative work.

One application that can be found in the industrial sector is training and simulation. Workers can practice and learn new skills and test new equipment and procedures in a safe and realistic environment, thanks to the Metaverse, which can provide such an environment. Because of this, there may be less need for costly and time-consuming testing and training of the body.

The Metaverse can also be used for prototyping and design, enabling businesses to test and iterate on new goods and systems in a virtual environment before committing to creating expensive physical prototypes. This saves businesses time and money. The development process may proceed more quickly as a result, and the likelihood of design faults may be reduced.

The Metaverse can be utilized for various purposes, including training, prototyping, and collaboration and communication amongst teams, regardless of where they are physically located. This can allow businesses to bring together groups of specialists from all over the world to collaborate on projects in real-time, enhancing communication and coordination.

Incorporating the Metaverse into the workings of the industrial sector can result in several positive side effects, including enhanced production, creativity, and efficiency. We should anticipate more disruption and transformation in these fields as many businesses begin to adopt and integrate metaverse technology.

Automotive Industry to Include Metaverse

The automotive industry is beginning to investigate the possibility of using the Metaverse to improve the design process, testing procedures, and overall customer experience.

The designing and prototyping processes are areas where the Metaverse may find application in the automobile sector. When compared to the use of actual prototypes, the creation of virtual prototypes in the Metaverse enables businesses to test and iterate new concepts more expediently and cost-effectively. The development process may proceed more quickly as a result, and the likelihood of design faults may be reduced.

It is also possible to use the Metaverse for testing and simulation. This will enable businesses to test new vehicle designs and systems in a virtual environment before committing to more expensive physical testing. It may shorten the time and resources required for testing while simultaneously increasing the level of safety associated with the procedure.

In addition to its use in design and testing, the Metaverse has the potential to be used to improve consumer experiences. An example would be enabling customers to virtually personalize and test drive vehicles in a realistic and immersive environment.

There is significant room for growth in the automotive industry's application of the Metaverse. Still, several problems and factors need to be kept in mind. In this context, "problems" refer to the cost and complexity of deploying metaverse technology and the requirement to secure the security and privacy of data and virtual assets. To be able to make use of the potential of this technology fully, these obstacles will need to be overcome as the use of the Metaverse in the automotive sector continues to expand.

Metaverse Stirs Up Software Development

As a result of the ongoing evolution and expansion of the Metaverse, there is an ever-increasing requirement for creating new programs and applications that can serve this online environment. This encompasses everything from apps tailored to specific industries or use cases to software that runs on the Metaverse platform.

The process of developing software for the Metaverse gives software developers a wide variety of options as well as problems. On the one hand, there is a considerable demand for brand-new metaverse software and a massive untapped market for both original and helpful applications. On the other side of the coin, designing software for the Metaverse calls for an in-depth knowledge of the technologies behind it, in addition to the fact that it can be complex and time intensive.

For software developers working in the metaverse area, there are many hurdles to overcome, not only in the realm of technology but also in the realms of commerce and law. These concerns include monetization, intellectual property protection, and user data confidentiality.

In general, software products for the Metaverse is a dynamic and fast-developing field with significant untapped potential for innovation and expansion. It is reasonable to anticipate that the field of software development will be home to an increasing number of fascinating breakthroughs and lucrative opportunities as the Metaverse progresses and develops.

The Age of Revolution for Telcos

The metaverse, a virtual community in which users may share and discuss digital content in real-time, has the potential to alter how we connect and conduct business ultimately. Telecommunications firms (or "telcos") stand at a critical juncture in their history since they can influence the future direction of the metaverse as it expands and develops. we will now look at where telcos are now, where they could go, what it would take to thrive in the burgeoning metaverse market, and what to keep in mind while doing so.

The potential of Telcos in the Metaverse

Telecommunications companies are already active in the Metaverse in several different ways. Many internet service providers now offer bundles of services that provide users with access to virtual reality (VR) and augmented reality (AR) content. Additionally, some internet service providers have formed partnerships with developers of Metaverses to provide specialized services within virtual environments. For instance, a telecommunications company may offer a virtual reality (VR) gaming package that allows users to access a selection of VR games in exchange for a monthly subscription fee. Alternatively, the company may collaborate with a Metaverse developer to provide in-game communication services such as voice and text chat.

In addition to these offers, telecommunications companies play an essential part in the Metaverse by supplying the fundamental infrastructure and connectivity required to access and use virtual environments. This includes items like broadband internet, mobile networks, and data centers, all of which are necessary for supporting high-bandwidth applications and services found in the Metaverse. Broadband internet, mobile networks, and data centers are all examples.

Despite their involvement in the Metaverse, telcos' primary role is primarily restricted to providing essential infrastructure and connections. A good number of telcos still need to embrace the promise of the Metaverse entirely and have yet to investigate new avenues for the creation of income and the engagement of customers.

Adapting to new technological developments and business models is one of the primary obstacles that telcos will need to overcome to increase their involvement in the Metaverse. Because the Metaverse is a domain that is constantly changing, telcos will need to ensure that they are always up to date on the most recent advancements in the field to maintain their relevance and competitiveness.

Investing in new infrastructures such as 5G networks or investigating the possibility of forming new alliances and collaborations with the producers of Metaverses and other participants in the sector will accomplish this goal. Telcos will need to be prepared to adapt to new revenue streams, such as the sale of virtual products or advertising within video games, to take full advantage of the potential given by the metaverse.

Regulatory compliance presents yet another obstacle for carriers operating in the Metaverse. New rules and regulations are expected to be enacted as it becomes increasingly integrated into day-to-day life. Laws and regulations will be implemented to govern actions that take place in virtual spaces and safeguard users. Telcos will be required to stay current on these developments and ensure they comply with all rules and regulations pertinent to their industry.

In retrospect, even though telecommunications companies already play an essential part in the metaverse, there is a sizable window of opportunity for them to broaden their involvement and impact in this dynamic and fast-developing field.

Of note, Telcos face several problems and opportunities posed by the Metaverse; yet to maintain their relevance in this quickly-developing arena, they must adapt and innovate. Using their knowledge and experience in connectivity and infrastructure, telcos can expand their product and service offerings in the Metaverse to include virtual reality services and real estate. On the other hand, telcos are confronted with rivalry, regulatory hurdles, and the imperative to stay abreast of advancing technology trends in the metaverse.

Telcos should investigate the possibility of entering into strategic alliances with other companies, developing new avenues of income, and investigating untapped consumer bases to improve their profitability prospects in the metaverse.

Key takeaways

The chapter on metaverse tools and technologies teaches us the following:

- Metaverse devices, such as virtual reality headsets and haptic gloves, are specialized techniques for entering and interacting with the Metaverse.
- At a bare minimum, you'll need a computer or game system and a metaverse device to enter the Metaverse. Your time spent in the Metaverse can be improved with the help of ancillary devices like motion controllers and virtual reality treadmills.
- Consider things like pricing, availability, comfort, the convenience of usage, and compatibility with your system while buying metaverse gear.
- Metaverse technologies include virtual reality, augmented reality, 3D graphics and rendering, motion tracking and haptic feedback, artificial intelligence and natural language processing, cloud computing and distributed networks, blockchain, decentralized technologies, and more.
- Training, prototyping, and cooperation in a virtual environment are all ways in which the usage of the Metaverse in the industrial sector might transform how businesses function.
- While some hurdles and considerations must be satisfied, the car industry is beginning to investigate the possibility of using the Metaverse to improve design, testing, and customer experiences.
- Opportunities and challenges, from the technological and financial to the legal and ethical, await software developers working in the As providers of connectivity and infrastructure,

telecommunications companies have the potential to play a crucial part in the metaverse.
- Telcos have several difficulties and opportunities brought on by the Metaverse.
- The only way telcos can remain relevant in the Metaverse and continue to adapt and innovate is to broaden their services, form strategic alliances with other businesses, and investigate untapped areas.

6

METAVERSE TRENDS AND PREDICTIONS

In recent years, the metaverse has attracted attention as a means of connecting with other people, conducting business, and even experiencing other worlds. For those interested in the future of the Metaverse and are looking ahead to the year 2023, several trends and predictions should be taken into consideration. We will discuss some of the most critical developments and forecasts for the metaverse in 2023 to include topics such as what businesses may realistically anticipate from the Metaverse, the role Metaverse development companies will play, and more.

Metaverse Predictions to Lookout for in 2023

We will address the proliferation of virtual reality technology and its increasing incorporation into the Metaverse. Although the technology behind virtual reality (VR) has been known for several decades, it has only very recently been more reasonably priced and become accessible to the general population. By 2023, virtual reality technology will have become more of a mainstream technology, offering a wider variety of uses inside the Metaverse.

Because users of VR technology will be able to interact with virtual worlds and objects more naturally and intuitively, full immersion experiences will be possible within the Metaverse thanks to the utilization of VR technology. Virtual reality can completely transform the Metaverse, turning it into a staging ground for various activities and forms of entertainment, such as games, movies, concerts, and more.

We may also anticipate the development of more powerful graphics and haptic technology, both of which will further enhance the level of realism and immersion that can be achieved within Metaverse experiences as VR technology becomes more widely adopted. As a result of these improvements, the Metaverse will develop into an alternative to the actual world that is even more appealing and lifelike.

The Emergence of Metaverse-Based Social Platforms and Communities

The Metaverse has already begun to function as a platform for socializing and engaging with others in virtual places. This trend will likely continue and even increase in the year 2023. As the Metaverse continues to advance in realism and immersion, it will one day serve as a primary channel for communication and interaction for specific individuals. The technology of virtual reality (VR), becoming increasingly affordable and accessible, will play a significant part in the process of creating the Metaverse as a more engaging social platform. With virtual reality (VR), users can interact with virtual environments and things more naturally and intuitively, giving the impression that they are in a real place.

We anticipate the establishment of virtual social platforms and communities within the Metaverse. These will be places where individuals can communicate with one another, share content, and build relationships in a purely digital environment. These online communities could take many forms, such as chat rooms in virtual reality, online forums, or even entire virtual towns where individuals can congregate and connect.

The expansion of these online communities can have a variety of different effects on the actual world. People will likely spend more time in the metaverse and less time connecting with others face-to-face. This could decrease the number of in-person social contacts and even cause communities to disappear entirely. On the other side, the Metaverse may also serve as a means by which individuals can connect with others who share their related interests and values, even if they are physically separated from one another.

In addition to offering a stage for interacting and making connections with other people, the Metaverse can provide a proving ground for novel concepts and ways of being. The experimentation of new social norms and behaviors, which might one day be implemented in the "real world," might be carried out in a "laboratory" setting within virtual communities. For instance, virtual communities could experiment with new types of government, new ways of arranging jobs, or new educational methods.

The creation of social platforms and communities built on Metaverses is a trend that will likely become more prevalent in 2023. These online communities can alter how we socialize and engage with one another, and they may even have a trickle-down effect on our world.

The Growth of the Metaverse Economy and the Emergence of Virtual Real Estate

As the metaverse gains in notoriety and realism, we anticipate an increase in the value of virtual products and services and increased commerce involving those commodities and services within the virtual world.

The economy of the Metaverse has the potential to develop into a substantial economic force, with people purchasing and selling virtual products and services in the same manner as in the real world. These virtual goods and services might include anything from virtual clothing and accessories to virtual real estate and even virtual experiences, such as virtual concerts or virtual adventure trips.

The emergence of virtual real estate is significant because it has the potential to become a new asset class in its own right. This makes the development of virtual real estate particularly notable. It is possible for people to buy and sell real estate within the Metaverse, just like they do in the real world with actual property. This may even contain virtual homes, land, and structures.

The traditional economy will likely be influenced in some way by virtual real estate's development and the Metaverse economy's expansion. First, it might open up new doorways for people to find ways to make a living inside the virtual world. In addition, the value of virtual assets might be connected to the value of assets in the actual world, adding an extra layer of complexity to the functioning of the global economy.

In general, the most important developments to keep an eye out for in 2023 are the expansion of the economy of the Metaverse and the advent of virtual real estate. These advancements should provide new economic opportunities and disrupt existing economic activity paradigms.

Metaverse integration with IoT, AI

The Internet of Things, sometimes known as IoT, is a technology that can significantly affect the Metaverse. The phrase "Internet of Things" (IoT) refers to the ever-expanding network of real-world goods, such as home appliances, motor cars, and even factory machinery that connect to the internet and exchange data. This network is known as the "Internet of Things." The Internet of Things (IoT) and the Metaverse will likely intersect in the not-too-distant future. At that point, it will be feasible to control and manipulate real-world things, even in a virtual environment.

For instance, a person may use their digital persona to start their car from within the Metaverse or turn on the lights in their home. This could have both practical and creative repercussions. It could enable people to control and monitor their home or office remotely and open the door to more creative possibilities, such as creating virtual reality games that incorporate real-world objects as set dressing.

Artificial Intelligence is another type of technology with the potential to mold the future of the Metaverse. There are diverse ways to enhance the practicality of the Metaverse and the experience of users. For instance, AI might be used to construct virtual surroundings that are more realistic and dynamic, and it could also be used to personalize the experience of using the Metaverse for each user. People would have an easier time interacting with and navigating the virtual world if AI were employed to power virtual assistants and other conversational agents within the Metaverse.

As 2023 progresses, one trend to keep an eye on is merging the Metaverse with other technologies like the IoT and AI. These technologies can generate new opportunities for interaction and control within the virtual realm and improve the functionality of the Metaverse and the user experience provided.

The role of smaller, independent studios in shaping the metaverse

A thriving ecosystem of smaller, independent development studios pushing the boundaries of what is possible within the virtual world, even though a few prominent players currently dominate the Metaverse industry. These studios are thrusting the boundaries of what is possible within the virtual world.

These more nimble and risk-taking smaller studios are a significant driving force in the Metaverse sector due to their greater agility, ability to take risks, and capacity to experiment with new concepts. They also have a greater propensity to concentrate on niche markets and specialized fields, such as the educational or medicinal applications of the Metaverse, for example.

In 2023, we anticipate seeing these more intimate studios continue contributing to sculpting the metaverse's future. They'll develop brand-new applications and experiences that cater to specific populations and solve particular challenges. They have the potential to act as a source of innovation and inspiration for the industry's more established companies as well.

A trend that will be important to watch in the Metaverse sector in 2023 is the involvement of smaller, independent development studios. These studios can encourage creativity and variety within the virtual world and offer new and original points of view.

What Businesses can Anticipate from the Metaverse in 2023

Businesses are beginning to take notice of the potential opportunities and difficulties presented by the Metaverse as it continues to grow and develop. This is because the Metaverse is a virtual environment. In 2023, we anticipate seeing organizations of all sizes and industries explore how they can harness it to reach new customers, adapt to new business methods, and drive innovation. This section will discuss the opportunities and challenges businesses will face in the Metaverse in 2023.

Opportunities for Businesses in the Metaverse

In 2023, one of the most significant opportunities enterprises can anticipate from is expanding their consumer base and entering new markets. Businesses will have the opportunity to reach a potentially large audience that consists of users of a variety of virtual worlds as the popularity of the Metaverse continues to rise and its accessibility improves. This might include those already well-versed in the Metaverse and people on the cusp of discovering this new and fascinating sphere for the first time. In the real world, businesses may need help to attract and keep clients as they may in the Metaverse by developing interactive and immersive experiences.

Businesses can anticipate gaining new consumers, adapting to new ways of conducting business, and connecting with customers in the Metaverse. In addition to this, businesses can anticipate expanding their customer base. In this context, "adopting" new technology and platforms to promote virtual commerce and communication and creating new strategies for marketing and customer engagement in the virtual world fall under this rubric. For enterprises to maintain their level of effectiveness and competitiveness in this arena amid the ongoing development of the Metaverse, they will need to be in alignment with the most recent developments in terms of both trends and innovations.

The possibility of using this virtual environment as a platform for teaching and cooperation, as well as invention, is a significant additional opportunity for firms operating in the Metaverse. Companies might use it as a platform for the virtual training and onboarding of new employees and the continued professional growth of existing staff members. Even if employees are located in different regions of the world, the Metaverse can make it easier for them to collaborate and work together as a team.

In addition, businesses can use the Metaverse as a testing ground for new concepts and prototypes before introducing them into the real world. This may be accomplished using the Metaverse as a space for experimentation and invention. In general, it offers a variety of chances for businesses to expand their operations and achieve greater levels of success in the digital sphere.

Challenges for Businesses in the Metaverse

Although the metaverse offers a variety of options for organizations, it is essential to consider the various obstacles that may appear in this virtual realm. The need to manage and comply with a wide variety of regulatory difficulties is likely to be one of the most significant obstacles that firms will encounter in the Metaverse. Governments and regulatory agencies may start developing laws and guidelines to govern activities in the virtual world as the Metaverse continues to expand and grow in the years to come. This may involve protecting personal information, data, intellectual property, and consumer rights. Businesses must be aware of these requirements and comply with them to prevent potential legal concerns.

Another potential obstacle that may be faced by firms operating in the Metaverse is the requirement to manage concerns around safety. Data breaches and cyber-attacks are risky because of the growing amount of personal and sensitive information exchanged in the virtual world. Businesses must install stringent security measures and educate their employees and customers on protecting themselves while navigating the Metaverse to defend themselves from these dangers.

In addition to concerns over regulations and safety, businesses may also need help navigating and competing in a virtual environment that is constantly changing. The Metaverse is a landscape that is continually shifting, as seen by the appearance of innovations and fashions regularly. For businesses to continue to be competitive and relevant in the Metaverse, they must keep themselves up to date and adapt to the changes occurring. This may involve a significant investment of time and resources and a willingness to embrace innovation and take risks.

When companies first join the realm of virtual reality, they will find that the Metaverse confronts them with a variety of obstacles. While it's true that these obstacles could be considered formidable, they also create opportunities for organizations to expand and adapt in an environment that's constantly shifting.

In summary, the Metaverse offers various opportunities and obstacles for enterprises in 2023. On one hand, businesses can anticipate expanding their client base and entering new markets due to the Metaverse. On the other hand, businesses will need to learn new ways to engage with customers and conduct business in the virtual world. The Metaverse allows organizations to exploit this virtual world for various purposes, including training, collaboration, and innovation. Companies will need to navigate and comply with multiple regulatory difficulties, handle security concerns, and adapt to the ever-changing terrain of the metaverse.

In general, the Metaverse presents enterprises with a one-of-a-kind and fascinating opportunity to investigate and enter a new market with the potential to be extremely large. The potential rewards of success in the Metaverse make it an intriguing place to follow in 2023 and beyond, even though there are undoubtedly issues to be solved in this space.

Metaverse Development Companies in 2023

Companies specializing in metaverse development play an essential part in its birth and evolution. These businesses are in charge of conceiving and constructing the future of this digital environment, in addition to developing the technologies, platforms, and experiences that go into making up the Metaverse.

The creation of virtual and augmented reality technologies is currently being worked on by businesses of varying sizes and concentrations, which has resulted in the Metaverse development sector that is rapidly increasing and evolving. These companies are on the cutting edge of innovation, exploring new ways for people to connect with and experience the metaverse in their products and services. Firms that produce virtual reality technology and software, companies that create interactive and immersive content for the metaverse, and companies that provide platforms and tools for developing and managing metaverse experiences, are all examples of companies that develop the Metaverse.

The industry of developing the metaverse is an exciting and dynamic sector that contains an infinite number of potential outcomes for the future of the metaverse.

Leading metaverse development companies

A significant number of businesses are actively attempting to mold the future of the Metaverse; nonetheless, a select few stand out as being very prominent and inventive within the sector. These pioneering metaverse development companies dictate the industry's course and are the primary forces behind producing fresh and engaging metaverse experiences.

The following are examples of leading companies in the field of Metaverse development:

- Oculus is a market leader in developing virtual reality gear and software. The company primarily focuses on producing high-quality, immersive virtual reality experiences. Facebook currently owns Oculus. Oculus has established a strong influence in the gaming and entertainment industries thanks to creating various successful virtual reality devices, such as the Oculus Rift and Oculus Quest headsets.
- Magic Leap is a leading innovator in the field of augmented reality. The firm is in charge of creating augmented reality (AR) technology and its related applications for many industries. The Magic Leap One headgear, which uses cutting-edge AR technology to superimpose digital objects and information onto the actual world, was just made available for purchase by the company Magic Leap.
- Unity Technologies is a frontrunner in producing interactive and immersive material for the metaverse, particularly in developing educational and training experiences. This firm is known as "Unity." Unity Technologies has earned a solid name in the gaming industry and the education and corporate training markets thanks to the creation of the Unity engine, a platform used extensively for the creation and execution of interactive 3D content.

These are only a few instances of the leading Metaverse development companies that are currently impacting the path the Metaverse will follow in the coming years.

Collaboration and partnerships with businesses

It is possible for enterprises that specialize in developing the Metaverse to collaborate with businesses operating in a wide variety of sectors in offering bespoke metaverse experiences or integrations. These partnerships have the potential to bring a variety of benefits to businesses. Some include engaging with customers in novel and immersive ways, using the metaverse for training and collaboration, and generating revenue through selling virtual goods and services within the Metaverse.

Several examples of successful partnerships between corporations and enterprises specialize in building metaverses. For instance, Oculus collaborated with Toyota to develop an employee virtual reality training program. This program has been shown to be an efficient and exciting way to train staff, and it was created with the help of Oculus. The partnership between Magic Leap and Lowe's resulted in creating an immersive virtual reality shopping experience for customers of both companies. This resulted in an increase in consumer happiness as well as customer loyalty. The National Basketball Association (NBA) and Unity Technologies have worked together to develop a virtual reality basketball training experience that players and coaches have positively accepted.

Future of metaverse development companies

The future of the metaverse seems promising, and organizations that specialize in developing the Metaverse will play an essential part in the formation of the digital world. These firms are continually developing new technologies and platforms, which will be the driving force behind the expansion of the Metaverse, and they are at the forefront of innovation.

The future of metaverse development companies is anticipated to be influenced by several trends and growth areas that are now being explored. The following are possible trends:

- The extension of the use of the metaverse beyond gaming and entertainment into other spheres of activity such as education, healthcare, and business.
- The introduction of new platforms and technology allows for creating metaverse content and interaction with that content.
- The increasing number of social and personal relationships made through the Metaverse, including the hosting of virtual events and meetings.
- The ever-increasing significance of compatibility across several platforms and interoperability in the Metaverse.

Key takeaways

In conclusion, this chapter has examined several important tendencies and forecasts about the metaverse in 2023:

- The anticipated expansion and development of the Metaverse will be driven by the soaring popularity of virtual reality and augmented reality technology and the introduction of new applications and uses across various business sectors.
- The opportunities the metaverse presents for businesses such as the expansion of possibilities for remote collaboration and communication, the utilization of the Metaverse for customer experiences and marketing, the potential for new revenue streams through the sale of virtual goods and services, and adapting to the shifting role that physical locations play in the Metaverse are all examples.
- The part companies specializing in the creation of the Metaverse will assist companies and individuals in navigating the complicated landscape of the Metaverse and capitalizing on the opportunities it presents.

The most important thing one should take away from this chapter is the realization that the Metaverse will likely be a rapidly expanding space in 2023. Businesses and individuals should be prepared to adapt to this virtual world's changing landscape to maximize any opportunities. This may entail keeping abreast of the most recent tendencies and advancements, collaborating with companies that specialize in the development of the Metaverse and contemplating how it can be utilized for things such as remote collaboration, improved customer experiences, and additional revenue streams.

7

THE METAVERSE AND THE FUTURE

In this chapter, we will discuss the probable future of the Metaverse and how it may affect several facets of our life such as our jobs, schools, and relationships with one another. We will examine why many industry professionals think the Metaverse is the future. We will also discuss this growing virtual environment's possible advantages and disadvantages. We will present a balanced and nuanced perspective of the Metaverse's role in creating our future by investigating forecasts in the year 2030 while thinking about the enthusiasm surrounding its potential development.

Why the Metaverse is the Future

As a potential future for how we will live and interact with one another, the idea of the Metaverse, a shared virtual space that blends the real world with the digital world, has been receiving increasing attention. The word "Metaverse" wasn't coined until the 1990s, but recent advancements in virtual reality (VR) and augmented reality (AR) technology have moved the concept much closer to becoming a reality.

The Metaverse can be conceptualized in its most basic form as a completely immersive and interactive online world. This is one way to explain it. It enables users to view and interact with a digital environment in a convincingly real and palpable way. Virtual reality (VR) or augmented reality (AR) devices, such as headsets or glasses, can be accessed. The Metaverse can completely transform how we do our jobs, interact with one another, and even gain access to information and entertainment.

The exponential growth in computing power and internet connectivity is one of the primary forces propelling Metaverse creation. Computers are becoming more and more powerful. The processing power and data storage capacity of modern computers and smartphones is substantially more than that of their forebears, enabling more realistic and sophisticated virtual experiences. Users can now quickly access and interact with the metaverse regardless of location, thanks to the widespread availability of high-speed internet access. This has made it possible for most of the world's population to participate in online activities.

The Metaverse will bring about significant changes in how we live our lives and connect as it continues to evolve and expand. We are going to probe into the potential benefits as well as the obstacles that the Metaverse as the future may present.

The role of computing power and internet connectivity in expanding the metaverse

The spread of the Metaverse and the development of more immersive virtual experiences are driven by significant developments in processing power and improvements in internet connectivity. The capacity of a computer or other device to process and otherwise work with data is referred to as computing power. The intricacy and sense of realism of virtual environments have expanded over the years alongside the advancements in processing power. Users can have the experience of being fully present in a virtual space thanks to the advent of high-performance computers and graphics processing units (GPUs), which are now capable of rendering realistic and lifelike virtual worlds in real-time.

In addition to improvements in processing power, the proliferation of high-speed internet connection across the globe has been an extremely significant contributor to the growth of the Metaverse. Users can communicate with one another and access virtual environments from any location because of the accessibility provided by the internet. This opens up the possibility of worldwide collaboration and communication within the Metaverse.

These technical breakthroughs have provided the groundwork necessary for the Metaverse to develop into an alternative to the real world that can be used for various activities and interactions. In the following section, we will discuss potential advantages the Metaverse may offer in the foreseeable future.

The potential benefits of the metaverse as the future

The Metaverse may offer a wide variety of advantages in the not-too-distant future, and there are a lot of them. The following are some of the most impressive benefits:

- The capacity to work remotely and participate in virtual meetings in the Metaverse can result in significant time and resource savings and remove the requirement to commute. This will lead to an increase in both efficiency and productivity. The Metaverse can also provide a flexible work

environment conducive to collaboration in virtual office spaces and coworking environments.
- Access to opportunities and resources on a global scale: The metaverse can provide access to opportunities and resources that may not be available in particular physical locales. By way of illustration, a student who lives in a more distant part of the country might use the Metaverse to gain access to the same educational opportunities and resources as a student who resides in a more populated location.
- New ways of expressing oneself creatively and artistically: The creation of virtual worlds, avatars, and other digital content can provide the Metaverse with the potential to introduce novel avenues for artistic and creative expression. Additionally, it can serve as a platform for artists and creators to share their work with an audience worldwide.

In general, the growth of the Metaverse can bring about substantial changes and improvements in various facets of our life, and these changes and enhancements are for the better. As the Metaverse development continues, we will move on to discuss potential obstacles and constraints that the Metaverse may encounter.

The Metaverse has the potential to bring about profound changes in how we live our lives and communicate with one another in the not-too-distant future. The integration of technologies such as virtual reality and augmented reality, as well as developments in computing power and internet connectivity, has the potential to make the Metaverse a game-changer in many facets of our lives, including jobs, schools, and our relationships.

It is essential to acknowledge that the growth and development of the Metaverse are not going to occur in a vacuum free of obstacles and constraints. As the Metaverse becomes more widespread, there will be a greater need to address ethical concerns such as protecting personal information and safety. The practical applications of the Metaverse may have their own set of limits, particularly in fields that demand a high level of presence in the actual world and connection with customers.

In the end, the success of the Metaverse will be contingent on growth and regulation in a responsible manner. If these problems can be solved efficiently, the Metaverse has the potential to live up to the hype that has been surrounding it and become an important force in determining the course of future events.

Metaverse: The Future of Work

The Metaverse carries the potential to bring about a sea change in the way that we operate and conduct business. The capacity to participate in meetings and work together with coworkers in a virtual setting from any location in the world is a significant advantage offered. This might result in a substantial gain in both productivity and efficiency because it would remove the requirement for actual travel and make it possible to maintain flexible work hours. In addition, virtual office spaces could become more widespread, making it possible to have a less and more adaptable centralized workplace. These shifts could significantly impact the conventional office paradigm of working from 9 to 5 and how we think about the workplace.

However, the impact of the Metaverse on work extends far beyond merely virtual meetings and collaboration. The creation of the Metaverse may give rise to new employment opportunities and sectors, such as the organization of virtual events and the development of the virtual real estate. As it evolves, new abilities and knowledge will likely be required to compete in the labor market. Those who wish to gain them will need to prepare themselves accordingly.

The Metaverse, as a whole, can bring about significant shifts in employment and the way we do business. The following sections explore a virtual workplace's potential benefits and challenges.

Virtual Meetings and Collaboration

Work done remotely will become more commonplace as the Metaverse grows and becomes more ingrained in our day-to-day lives. It would be simpler for people to work from anywhere if they could participate in meetings and work on projects electronically with coworkers as mentioned. This significantly boosts flexibility and makes it possible to form more diverse and scattered teams.

On the other hand, the growing reliance on virtual communication and collaboration brings with it a unique set of difficulties. Working remotely can make it more challenging to form personal connections and earn the trust of coworkers. In addition, problems may arise due to the disparity in time zones and difficulty in developing a cohesive team culture.

On the other hand, many potential benefits may be gained from working in a virtual environment. It has been demonstrated that working remotely increases both productivity and job satisfaction. This is likely because one can maintain a healthier work-life balance and the flexibility to work from a place better suited to their requirements. People who live in more rural or remote places and those with physical limitations may find it simpler to engage in the workforce thanks to the Metaverse.

In general, the Metaverse can significantly alter the future of work and how we conduct business, both in terms of increased connectivity and collaboration, as well as the potential challenges and benefits of a virtual workplace. This can be classified into two categories: (1) increased connectivity and collaboration and (2) potential challenges and benefits of a more virtual workplace.

New Job Opportunities and Industries

In addition to the possibility of holding meetings online and carrying out work remotely, the Metaverse may also steer the development of new lines of employment and enterprises. There may be a demand for virtual event planners who can create and oversee the management of events within the Metaverse. There may also be a demand for virtual real estate developers who can create and manage various virtual spaces.

The emergence of the Metaverse may result in establishing new business sectors that are not even conceivable to us. It is challenging to anticipate precisely what the future will hold for each newly-developed technology. Furthermore, it cannot be denied that the Metaverse has the potential to impact the labor market and produce new employment prospects significantly.

we will now discuss a more virtual workplace's potential advantages and disadvantages in the Metaverse. However, before we get into this, it is essential to consider how the Metaverse can alter the skills and knowledge needed to advance in the labor market. As the Metaverse continues to grow and become more integrated into our day-to-day lives, new jobs and sectors will arise that we cannot even conceptualize.

The Future of Remote Work

Work done remotely will become more commonplace as the Metaverse grows and becomes more ingrained in our day-to-day lives. However, even though it can boost flexibility and make it possible for more varied and geographically-dispersed teams, it also offers its own unique set of obstacles. We will examine a virtual workplace's potential advantages and difficulties in the Metaverse.

Productivity gains and overall job satisfaction are the two main upsides of transitioning to a more virtual work environment. Studies have indicated that employees who work from home tend to be more productive and have a higher level of job satisfaction than their colleagues who work in an office setting. This could result from several things, including a more favorable work-life balance and the opportunity to perform one's job in an environment better suited to the individual's particular requirements and preferences. The Metaverse has the potential to increase accessibility and inclusivity by making it more straightforward for those with impairments or who live in remote places to engage in the workforce.

However, there are also possible difficulties associated with working in a more virtual environment. When you work remotely with your coworkers, developing personal connections and earning their trust might become more challenging. In addition, problems may arise due to the disparity in time zones and difficulty in developing a cohesive team culture. These difficulties will need to be addressed for a more virtual workplace to be successful.

The Metaverse, as a whole, can bring about significant shifts in employment and the way we do business. The potential advantages of a more virtual workplace make moving toward one an intriguing one for the future, despite the obstacles to be surmounted.

In short, the Metaverse can ultimately transform how we operate and conduct business. Productivity and efficiency could be significantly improved if workers could participate in meetings and communicate with coworkers electronically, regardless of location. The creation of the Metaverse may give rise to new employment opportunities and sectors, such as the organization of virtual events and the development of virtual real estate.

A workplace that is increasingly virtual has the potential to promote flexibility while also allowing for more diverse and geographically dispersed teams. However, there is the possibility of encountering obstacles, such as difficulties in forming personal connections and creating trust with coworkers when working remotely. These obstacles must be overcome.

The Metaverse can bring about significant shifts in employment and the way we do business. Although there may be obstacles to overcome, the opportunities that may arise making this an exciting prospect for the future. It will be interesting to observe how it develops over the next several years because it has the possibility to have a significant impact on a variety of work fields areas of everyday life.

Why Does it Matter that the Metaverse is Expanding?

The Metaverse has the potential to impact society as a whole as well as how we go about living our daily lives. Individuals can connect and speak with others regardless of their location thanks to the Metaverse, which serves as a platform for social interaction and connection in a virtual environment. This can result in the formation of online communities and foster the opportunity to develop personal relationships and social links with individuals residing in other parts of the world.

The Metaverse not only has the potential to become a platform for social interaction, but it also can alter how we take in information and enjoy ourselves in the entertainment world. It presents a new potential for participatory and immersive experiences, such as virtual reality gaming and virtual concerts. These opportunities are made possible by the fact that we can submerge ourselves in virtual worlds.

In addition, the Metaverse can bring about a revolution in teaching and education. In recent years, virtual classrooms and online education have grown more common. However, the Metaverse can take this to a new level by creating a learning environment that is wholly immersive and participatory. Students can actively participate in virtual field trips, carry out experiments in virtual labs, and engage in one-on-one conversations with their instructors and fellow students within a virtual environment.

Economic impact

The proliferation of the Metaverse has the potential to stimulate economic expansion and produce new job openings.

People who can design and construct virtual worlds and can create virtual experiences and give technical assistance will be in high demand as it becomes increasingly used both by individuals and businesses. As firms and individuals look to the Metaverse as a platform for commerce and the exchange of goods and services, it also has the potential to disrupt old sectors and create new ones. This could lead to the creation of new industries altogether.

If the Metaverse is fully developed, people can visit virtual representations of real-world sites and wholly made-up places. This will make the concept of virtual tourism possible. It might even lead to the establishment of virtual places visitors visit and generate economic benefits due to people spending money on virtual experiences and virtual items.

It is necessary to think about how the Metaverse could disrupt conventional sectors and develop new ones as it expands and adapts. It is also essential to analyze the possible economic impact of the Metaverse as it continues to grow.

Importance of keeping up with advancements in metaverse technology

Individuals and businesses must stay up with the breakthroughs made in Metaverse technology as the Metaverse continues to grow and change. Early adopters may have a competitive edge since they can investigate and experiment with new virtual experiences and technology before they become more mainstream, giving them an advantage over later adopters.

As the Metaverse continues to advance, we must consider the ethical repercussions of this trend and the possibility of gaining a market edge. Technology that creates virtual realities raises concerns about invasions of privacy, the need for informed permission, and the possibility of sexual misconduct in a simulated environment. It is essential to consider these concerns carefully and ensure that the growth of and interaction with the Metaverse are conducted responsibly and ethically.

The Metaverse in 2030

The future state of the Metaverse in 2030 serves as this section's primary topic of discussion. The Metaverse is a virtual environment built and maintained by humans and technology. It has the potential to transform how we connect in addition to how we interact with technology. It is imperative that, as the Metaverse continues to grow and become more intertwined with our day-to-day lives, we carefully analyze what this prospective future may include and the effects it may have on various fields of endeavor.

In this section, we will discuss the potential technical breakthroughs that may contribute to the evolution of the Metaverse. We will cover the potential difficulties and disadvantages that may arise from these advancements. We will also investigate the potential advantages and prospects that the Metaverse may provide in the year 2030, as we think about its ability to bring about a significant good change in the world.

Predictions for the Metaverse in 2030

There is a good chance that considerable changes will have been made to the Metaverse by the year 2030 as a result of developments in technology such as virtual reality and Artificial Intelligence. These technical improvements might make it possible to have an experience in a virtual world that is both more immersive and participatory.

The way we work could also be revolutionized due to the Metaverse, leading to the widespread adoption of practices such as working from home or virtual workplaces. This may affect various businesses, including the real estate and transportation sectors.

The Metaverse may also significantly impact the entertainment business, especially if virtual concerts, festivals, and other events become more commonplace. It may also change the educational system, leading to the proliferation of online courses and virtual classrooms.

In general, the growth of the Metaverse in 2030 has the potential to have a significant impact on a wide range of different companies and sectors.

Potential Challenges and Drawbacks

There is a possibility that difficulties and disadvantages will emerge due to the expansion and increasing presence of the Metaverse in our everyday lives. Privacy and safety are two concerns that come to mind when thinking about the online world. There is an increased likelihood of data breaches and cyber-attacks due to the increased online sharing of personal and sensitive information.

The widespread adoption of the Metaverse may negatively influence specific industries or ways of life and cause these to be upended. For instance, the growing prevalence of employment-related applications of virtual reality and the Metaverse may result in the demise of particular physical businesses or a shift in the job market.

It is essential to address the potential difficulties and downsides that may arise to guarantee a bright and safe future for the metaverse.

THE METAVERSE AND THE FUTURE

Potential Benefits and Opportunities

The extension of the Metaverse may provide difficulties and disadvantages in the year 2030; yet there is also the possibility that it will present various advantages and chances. Because it is possible for people in different regions to quickly communicate with one another and work together in the virtual world, one potential advantage is a greater sense of global interconnectedness.

The Metaverse also can democratize specific industries by creating a level playing field and offering equal chances for all players. This can be accomplished by establishing a level playing field. For instance, the Metaverse may make it possible for more diverse and independent creators to achieve fame and success in the entertainment industry.

The Metaverse can bring about considerable change worldwide by enhancing communication, collaboration, and accessibility. In short, the Metaverse can bring about enormous changes in how we connect and conduct our lives in 2030. Developments in technology, such as virtual reality and Artificial Intelligence may contribute to the progress of the metaverse and make it possible to have an experience that is both more immersive and participatory. The Metaverse may alter the way we operate and have an effect on a variety of industries and markets.

However, to ensure a bright and safe future for the virtual world, it is essential to consider the potential difficulties and downsides posed by the Metaverse, such as concerns over privacy and security, and to work toward finding solutions. On the other hand, we must not lose sight of the myriad advantages and prospects that the Metaverse may present, such as a heightened sense of connection on a global scale and the democratization of particular fields of endeavor.

In general, the Metaverse will bring about tremendous beneficial change in the world; it will be intriguing to observe how it develops and evolves over the next few years.

Can Metaverse Live up to the Hype?

In recent years, the Metaverse has been the subject of a great deal of attention and enthusiasm, with many individuals anticipating that it will substantially impact various elements of our lives shortly. Some people and businesses have envisioned a future in which the Metaverse becomes the preeminent platform for communication, entertainment, and even work because of the idea of a virtual reality fully integrated with our actual world.

This idea has captured the imagination of both individuals and businesses. Just like with any other emerging technology, there are a lot of questions and worries regarding whether or not the Metaverse will live up to expectations. Will it make a significant difference in how we work and live, or will it fall short of expectations? In the following section, we will investigate these concerns and discuss the opportunities and obstacles presented by the Metaverse.

The Potential of the Metaverse

Many individuals believe that in the not-too-distant future, we will come to regard the Metaverse as an essential component of our everyday lives. It possesses a vast and varied potential to be used in various ways. The following is a brief list of how the Metaverse may have the potential to transform how we live and work:

- People will be able to engage in a virtual world as if they were in the exact physical location, thanks to

the Metaverse, which has the potential to make communication with other people a more immersive and realistic experience. This might be especially helpful for people who work remotely or have relationships separated by a long distance.
- Collaboration: The Metaverse has the potential to serve as a platform for virtual meetings and collaboration. This would make it possible for groups to work together in a virtual setting as if in the exact physical location. The possibility exists that this will make work done remotely more effective and productive.
- Virtual experiences and simulations give a more immersive and engaging way to have fun, which could be one of the new and exciting forms of entertainment that the Metaverse can offer in the future.
- Education: The Metaverse has the potential to be used for training and education, with virtual simulations and experiences giving a more dynamic and exciting method to learn.

These are just a few instances of the potential the Metaverse possesses; it is likely that as it continues to evolve, it will have even more far-reaching implications.

Challenges to Overcome
Despite its potential, the Metaverse still has a great deal of work to do before it can live up to the expectations that have been set. Among these difficulties:

- Technical constraints: Because the technology underpins the Metaverse and is still in its formative

stages, many technical constraints must be resolved. There are problems with latency and resolution, as well as the requirement for more powerful gear, all obstacles standing in the way of totally realistic virtual experiences.
- Regulatory issues: The Metaverse raises several concerns regarding regulatory matters, particularly privacy, intellectual property, and user safety. Before the Metaverse can develop to its full potential, these issues will need to be resolved.
- Trust and safety: For the Metaverse to become a popular platform, its users must be assured that their data and other personally identifiable information are safe and shielded from potential risks. The success of the Metaverse will be directly proportional to how successfully trust and safety can be established within it.

It will likely be some time before all of these concerns are adequately addressed because overcoming these obstacles will be essential to the development of the Metaverse. On the other hand, the potential of the metaverse cannot be denied, and it should be an exciting development to witness as it progresses.

It is challenging to provide an accurate forecast of how the Metaverse will evolve and what its eventual effects will be. The technology is still in its early phases of development, and there are many obstacles to conquer before it can truly live up to the hype. On the other hand, the potential of the metaverse cannot be denied, and it will be an exciting development to witness as it progresses.

The Metaverse can change how we live and work, but the answer to whether or not it will live up to the hype surrounding it will only be found over time. It remains to be seen if it finally becomes the dominating platform for communication, entertainment, and work. Still, the prospect that it will become such is undoubtedly interesting to think about. As the Metaverse continues to expand and mature, it will be fascinating to observe the horizon for the innovative new technology that is already available.

Key takeaways

The chapter has outlined the following hypothetical developments in the metaverse:

- As technology becomes more pervasive and sophisticated, the Metaverse stands to become a significant force in influencing the future.
- Through the utilization of virtual offices and meetings and the establishment of new employment markets within the Metaverse, it can transform how we work, communicate, and engage with one another.
- Increased global connectivity and communication and eliminating obstacles between individuals of different locations are possible outcomes of the Metaverse's development.
- While the Metaverse has enormous potential, it is fraught with difficulties and should be developed and adopted with prudence.

The main takeaway is that the Metaverse is a complicated and quickly changing technology with far-reaching implications for the future. Still, its development and acceptance must be approached with awareness of the risks and benefits involved.

Dear Reader,

As independent authors, it's often difficult to gather reviews compared with much bigger publishers.

Therefore, please leave a review on the platform where you bought this book.

KINDLE:

LEAVE A REVIEW HERE < click here >

Many thanks,

Author Team

CONCLUSION

We have defined the Metaverse as a virtual shared space in the first chapter. This space has been produced by converging virtually amplified physical reality and physically persistent virtual space. The Metaverse comprises all virtual worlds, augmented reality, and the internet. In addition, we investigated the background of the Metaverse as well as its development over time. We located its beginnings in the early virtual reality and online gaming systems and have explored the many guises it has assumed in the current day.

In the second chapter, we covered the numerous ways in which individuals and organizations might invest in the Metaverse. These ways include engaging in virtual economies, purchasing virtual assets and property, and investing in related enterprises. Additionally, we investigated the potential financial gains and the dangers linked with these investments.

In the third chapter, we discussed the advantages and disadvantages of the Metaverse. Specifically, we focused on the Metaverse's ability to open new avenues for business, entertainment, learning, and social interaction. On the other hand, the Metaverse might provide difficulties regarding privacy, safety, and government oversight.

In the fourth chapter, we discussed the numerous prospects for business made available by the Metaverse. Options include the development of virtual real estate, the creation of virtual goods and services, and the provision of Metaverse infrastructure. We also discussed the opportunities for businesses to leverage the Metaverse as a foundation for marketing and engaging with their customers.

In the fifth chapter, we dove deeper into the technologies and gadgets driving Metaverse creation. Some examples of these technologies and devices include augmented reality glasses, virtual reality headsets, and haptic interfaces. We also explored the function that Artificial Intelligence would play and the possibility that fifth-generation wireless networks will be able to meet the high bandwidth requirements.

In the sixth chapter, we discussed the potential impact of the Metaverse on the telecommunications industry. Specifically, we looked at how telcos can leverage the metaverse to offer new services and revenue streams and the challenges they may face in the process.

In the final chapters, we looked at current trends and made projections about the Metaverse's future. Topics discussed include the possibility that the metaverse will become an integral part of people's everyday lives, the emergence of new virtual social spaces, and the opportunity that the Metaverse will act as a platform for innovation and creativity.

Throughout the book, several recurring ideas have surfaced that bring to light the possibilities offered by the Metaverse as well as its significance.

Of note, it may completely transform many different businesses as well as society as a whole. It presents fresh possibilities for business, entertainment, learning, and social interaction, and it can revolutionize how we work, play, and communicate with one another. The Metaverse has already begun to make inroads in these areas, with companies using virtual and augmented reality for training and customer engagement and virtual social spaces like Second Life and VR Chat gaining popularity as places to hang out and meet new people.

These are just two examples of how the Metaverse has already begun to make inroads in these areas. As it continues to advance, it will have an increasingly more significant influence on our everyday lives and how we engage with the surrounding environment.

The significance of comprehending and considering the numerous prospects and dangers associated with the Metaverse is yet another essential idea. Although it presents users with fascinating opportunities, the Metaverse is full of difficulties. As it expands, significant challenges such as privacy, security, and regulation are becoming increasingly urgent and require immediate attention. Before plunging into the Metaverse, individuals and organizations need to consider these problems seriously to reduce the possibility of adverse outcomes while simultaneously increasing the likelihood of favorable results.

In conclusion, the Metaverse is an area that is continuously advancing. It is essential to continue evaluating and monitoring trends and changes to maintain one's knowledge and make judgments based on it. Maintaining a high awareness of the most recent trends and projections is essential for staying ahead of the competition and making the most of new opportunities. For the Metaverse to become more widespread, it will be necessary to keep up to date on emerging technologies.

Overarchingly, these recurrent themes stress the importance of being aware of and ready for the Metaverse's many opportunities and difficulties, as well as the potential to drastically alter how we live our lives and interact with the rest of the world.

The future of the Metaverse is rife with opportunities, and it will likely continue to develop and transform in ways we are presently unable to foresee completely. Nevertheless, a few possible developments are highly probable. There is a distinct possibility that the Metaverse will soon be an accepted and normalized component of the lives of a significant number of people. An increasing number will likely use the Metaverse for various purposes, including entertainment, education, and socialization.

As the technology behind virtual and augmented reality advances and becomes more widely available, this trend will likely continue. One day, firms will use the Metaverse for employee training, meetings, and other activities relevant to the business. This would make the Metaverse an even more critical part of the workplace.

The Metaverse may usher in brand-new societal and commercial engagement modes. People will be able to shop, interact with companies, and experience goods and services in new and exciting ways thanks to the combination of virtual reality and augmented reality. In addition, the Metaverse has the potential to supply new platforms for interacting with other people and forming connections with them, potentially supplanting or supplementing the function of virtual social spaces.

In conclusion, the Metaverse has the potential to act as a hub for innovation and creativity by furnishing people with new resources and environments in which they can generate and discuss original thoughts and experiences. People from various regions and walks of life can work together on projects and find solutions to problems in a new way thanks to the Metaverse, which also makes it possible for new kinds of collaboration and problem-solving to emerge.

Overall, the future of the Metaverse is exciting and full of potential, and it will likely continue to shape and be shaped by how we live our lives and interact with the world. In short, the future of the Metaverse is exciting and full of possibilities.

As we have discovered in this book, the Metaverse signifies a fundamental change in how we live and connect with the people around us and the wider world. It presents fresh possibilities for business, entertainment, learning, and social interaction, and it can revolutionize how we work, play, and communicate with one another.

Nevertheless, it is essential to approach the Metaverse with curiosity, prudence, and openness to the possibility of new experiences. Careful consideration must be given to the myriad of opportunities and threats that the Metaverse affords because, even though it presents a plethora of fascinating possibilities, it is full of difficulties. Individuals and companies must approach it with privacy, security, and regulation in mind, as these concerns need to be tackled as the Metaverse continues to expand.

Many questions remain about the Metaverse's future, but one thing is sure: it can dramatically alter our lives and future world. As the Metaverse develops and gains a broader audience, it will become vital to educate ourselves on the most recent trends and developments to take advantage of new opportunities and successfully handle any problems that may emerge. This is because it will be increasingly harder to distinguish between real and virtual worlds.

www.ingramcontent.com/pod-product-compliance
Lightning Source LLC
LaVergne TN
LVHW041639060526
838200LV00040B/1636